Penguin Garden Centre Guides

Labour-saving Gardening

Tom Wright

MAGNA BOOKS

This edition published 1992 by Magna Books, Magna Road,
Leicester, UK LE8 2ZH. Produced by the Promotional
Reprint Company Limited.

ISBN 1 85422 322 4

Edited and designed by Robert Ditchfield Ltd
Illustrated by Emma Tovey

Acknowledgements
The publishers would like to thank the following contributors and
copyright owners of the colour photographs:
Pat Brindley (40, 41); Martyn Rix (44); Diana Saville (17, 21 left, 29,
33, 37 above and below, 57, 61 right).

Printed & bound in Hong Kong

Contents

1. Garden Planning

Planning gardens is rather like planning the living room in houses, bringing order, purpose and beauty into what can so easily be muddle and confusion. A well planned garden has style and character and a sense of purpose and may be surprisingly simple in its design.

Before planning a completely new garden, or re-planning an existing one, study other gardens – large and small – for ideas, use of plants and the way they are planned. Labour saving is going to be the theme all through this book, so look out also for features that seem labour-intensive or labour-saving.

Next time you visit the Royal Horticultural Society's gardens at Wisley, in Surrey, go and see the various show gardens, especially plants for small gardens with different uses.

Three stages in planning

1 Draw a simple plan of your garden to a suitable scale to include the house and all boundaries, and also showing important features, if any, such as trees, paths or hedges that you want to keep. Then look at the check list opposite and read the appropriate pages in this book. Consider carefully the features and kinds of planting you would like to introduce to produce an attractive but labour-saving garden. You will also find it helpful to visit your local Garden Centre to see the materials and plants described in this book, compare their prices and ask advice about gardening in your area.

2 Now draw up a rough plan of all the important features not present in the existing garden that you wish to include, remembering that gardens with too many features can look overcrowded and can be much more difficult to maintain. Note the following features in the rough plan below:
Trees – Always think carefully before removing trees. They take a long time to replace.
Lawns – Reduce the number of small areas of grass.
Screen – For more privacy replace the open fence with a screen (pages 22–23).
Patio – A place to sit and enjoy the garden.

3 Draw a new plan for the garden showing the alterations you wish to make and fitting in the new features. Try making several different quick sketch plans before you arrive at the final one that satisfies most of your requirements. In the plan emphasise special features or points of interest. Avoid too many pieces of lawn, or do away with grass altogether. There may be sunny and shady, sheltered and windy, damp and dry places which will also affect your decisions. The garden below is not labour-free – no garden can be – but it incorporates features most people want in a labour-saving layout.

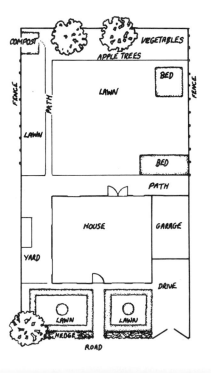

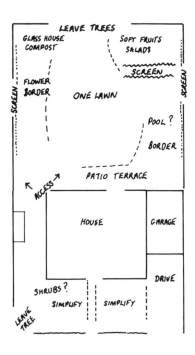

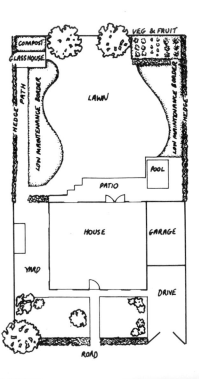

Low-maintenance gardens

The secret of planning a low-maintenance garden is the time and thought you spend on the planning stages. It will be a combination of a realistic layout and a careful choice of features and plants and a use of the proper techniques to look after the garden that will determine its success. Cost comes into this planning stage, since, unless you are a handyman, most of the low-maintenance constructed features like walls, paving, patios, gravel and the like are more expensive to buy than plants, but of course save in the sweat and toil of upkeep in the long run.

The check list below is a guide to the kind of decisions you must make when including various features in your plan. Further information appears in subsequent pages.

LABOUR INTENSIVE	LABOUR SAVING
LAWNS	
Close cut lawns containing rye grass (*Lolium perenne*).	Lawns which include creeping red fescue (*Festuca rubra* strains), no rye grass and not cut below 1 in (25mm).
HEDGES	
Fast growing kinds may need cutting up to four times a year – e.g. privet (*Ligustrum ovalifolium*), *Lonicera nitida*, Myrobolan plum (*Prunus cerasifera*). They may also be shorter lived.	These slow-growing, long-lived kinds usually need cutting only once or perhaps twice a year – yew (*Taxus baccata*), Lawson cypress (*Chamaecyparis lawsoniana*), beech (*Fagus sylvatica*), hornbeam (*Carpinus betulus*).
ROSES	
Hybrid tea and floribunda roses need regular pruning, pest and disease control and weed control.	Shrub roses – occasional pruning, very few pest and disease problems, will grow in grass or ground cover.
FLOWERS AND SHRUBS	
Annuals for summer display – spring planting, autumn lifting, regular weeding.	Heathers, flowering ground-cover shrubs, dwarf conifers etc. Very little attention needed after two or three years once established.
CLIMBERS	
Those needing support and pruning – e.g. roses, some clematis, wistaria. Regular maintenance essential.	Self-clinging or easy maintenance – Boston Ivy, Virginia creeper (if room), ivies, some clematis.
ROCK PLANTS	
Rockeries and rock gardens.	Raised beds, dry walls and terraces.

A cool, shaded garden of quite modest size presented the designer with a challenge which was to select a limited range of plants with strong leaf form and colours. Flowers have been restricted to white or very pale pink or yellow and blended associations create all the year round effect and quite low maintenance. Hostas thrive in cool shade provided the roots do not get too dry but the bare patches they leave in the winter need the winter clothing of such low cover evergreens as ivies, periwinkles, prostrate cotoneasters or the winter-green species of hellebores. A small garden like this could easily become overcrowded with a blur of too many plants.

A tapestry or 'maquis' boskage planting design, a complete ground-covering blend of shrubs and conifers for all year round effects and very little maintenance for many years. The secret here is to know one's soil and microclimate and then to pick those subjects like heathers, dwarf azaleas, and slow-growing conifers that do not fight too aggressively among themselves for living space, but seem to grow happily in a colourful community in a contrasted fashion. The occasional clipping after flowering is all many of these plants need and if the conifers seem to be growing excessively, light trimming in the growing season can soon restore their shape. Stepping stones or gravel, sawdust or shredded bark paths can be laid.

2. Use of Hard Materials

The most effective way to save labour is to make use of what are known as hard or constructed materials – namely, paving, stone or bricks. These should form the basis of the garden; and, if properly selected and assembled, the features they form will last for many years requiring the minimum attention.

Surfacing materials

Paving   Natural stone or composition slabs, crazy or random laid.

Bricks and setts   Fired bricks or natural stone or granite setts.

Concrete   Scope for different finishes or uses.

Macadam   Harsh and institutional for most gardens, except drives.

Pebbles, gravel, shingle   Plenty of scope, grades and finishes.

Comments

Long-lasting, but stone can be expensive. More permanent if laid in mortar.

More quality and character, especially in old gardens. Expensive but long-lasting. Weeds can colonise unless laid in mortar.

Quick, effective, economic and attractive if used with imagination at outset. Weed-proof.

Flexible surfacing for contours and slopes. Best for drives if well laid. Weed-proof. Beware of amateur operators.

Flexible and more in keeping with traditional garden paths and drives. Cheap, easily laid, but need regular weed treatment.

Materials for constructed features

Stone   Cut or dressed natural stone of the region.

Bricks   Traditional or engineering.

Composition stone or blocks   Now many styles and clever effects.

Wood   For outdoor uses, should always be seasoned and treated.

Comments

Expensive, but long-lasting for special walls, steps and other purposes. Retaining stone walls for alpine beds etc. (see pages 28–29).

The most attractive and permanent material for walls, steps, raised beds. Costly but long-lasting and very low maintenance.

Useful and effective when natural stone too expensive or difficult to obtain. Similar uses to stone or bricks. Low maintenance and reasonable costs.

Fences, screens, pergolas or raised beds, containers and retaining walls. Cheap. Unseasoned wood is a false economy. Sawn timber is cheaper, and railway sleepers ideal if still obtainable.

Raised beds

Raised beds of wood, stone, brick or even fibre-glass provide seating and effective retaining walls for plant associations. Paving or hard surfacing around them gives a functional, low-maintenance finish.

Costs

In comparison with the plants used in gardens, these materials can be very expensive but should be regarded as a middle or long-term investment. The better the class of materials, if carefully selected and sited, the better will be the design and finish and correspondingly the lower the maintenance afterwards. As already indicated there is a considerable difference in the comparative costs as the following table shows (these are 1985 prices).

Material	Approximate cost
Chippings/gravel 2 in (5 cm) deep	£1.00 per sq m
Concrete	£5.00 per sq m
Macadam	£8.00 per sq m
Paving slabs	£8.00 per sq m
Loose cobbles	£15.00 per sq m
Bricks and setts	£25.00 per sq m
York stone paving	£50.00 per sq m

Uses

As these hard materials are usually the framework and the most labour-saving component of gardens, then the greater area they cover (as opposed to the more labour-intensive mown grass or planted areas) the lower will be the overall upkeep. Always remember the importance of striking a balance between these hard elements and the softer planted ones, unless the intention is for a hard, utilitarian approach. For surfacing and for walls and steps, try to choose materials that match the house. Avoid bright hard colours unless the garden is really avant-garde! Paths, terraces and patios are usually the most common hard elements of most gardens, linking the different parts and also providing good firm surfaces that readily dry out after rain, and that also stand up to the same wear and tear, especially in winter and in wet spells. Worn turf can be dealt with once and for all by replacing it with a suitable hard material.

Be inventive with choosing and using paving materials. Paving slabs come in many different sizes and colours and the smaller sizes, although more expensive, will look better in smaller gardens.

Use small slabs or concrete strips as mowing margins to flank borders or walls beside mown grass. When grass meets hard surface, a neater, maintenance-free finish can be obtained by keeping the finished grass level ½ in (12 mm) above the path, as shown in the illustrations here.

Loose gravel chippings or crushed shingle make cheap, effective, low-maintenance surfaces for paths, drives and also for dry gardens, but when these meet grass some protective edging is important to stop the gravel encroaching on the grass and damaging mower blades. A metal band is probably the easiest to lay, as shown in the illustration on the right, but tiles or bricks are also suitable.

Mowing strip

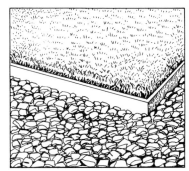
Edging strip

An attractive pattern of bricks and paving. Note the well-matched grass finish and the compact salads border.

3. Gardens for the Elderly and Disabled

Gardening, and the growing of plants are ideal activities for those who are either temporarily or permanently disabled, or simply getting less mobile and more infirm through old age. The day-by-day care of plants is rewarding and therapeutic, providing endless fascination. Plants, like people, also respond to regular loving care. But there is a limit to the effort and labour the elderly or the infirm can muster, and therefore a garden will have to be adapted or designed with this in mind. The following are some useful points to think about.

Designing or adapting the garden

1. **Access surfaces** like paths, patios and drives should be as smooth and even textured as possible with a minimum of steps and abrupt changes of level or preferably with ramps and gentle slopes for wheelchairs or those with walking aids, sticks etc.

2. **Grass areas** are nice to sit on, but there is the difficulty of mowing, so reduce this to an acceptable minimum; use mowing strips to cut down all that edging or replace with attractive paving or textured hard material (see pages 6–7).

3. **Raised beds** are ideal for all types of disabled gardeners and especially those with back troubles, when bending becomes painful. Adjust the height and width to suit those who are going to use them and give some variety of character to the levels to avoid them looking too institutional. Timber is cheaper and more adaptable than stone or bricks for making

A simple raised bed of treated timber.

Partially raised beds in a neat, well designed setting that elderly people can manage.

different structures. Design these to make nice enclosures but always make them easily accessible.

4. **Shelter** from chill winds and draughts is very important, so therefore use good, solid, boundary hedges or flowering shrubs or fences to create comfortable and secluded places for those who are going to spend many hours sitting or only moving slowly in the garden. When making living screens, choose hedges that need less frequent cutting (see pages 22–23) and try not to use the prickly or spiny types. Otherwise, use massed shrubs or conifers that need little or no pruning or trimming.

5. **Water** is fascinating to everyone and a raised pool can provide endless pleasure, as well as reducing the risk of accidents. Adding a small fountain brings the sound of water to the pool and this can also be enjoyed by blind gardeners, whom we must not forget in this chapter.

A raised pool requires less bending.

Plants

There is endless scope here depending on the tastes or preferences of the gardener, the degree of his/her infirmity and the size of the garden. It is important, however, when choosing plants and planting schemes, to consider labour-saving aspects. Here are some ideas:

Vegetables can be kept in small accessible beds which are raised if necessary. Select the more easily grown and more easily harvested types like lettuces, onions, runner beans etc. (see pages 34–35). Herbs like chives, parsley and sage can be grown as edging.

Fruit trees can be included if they are dwarf, trained trees on suitable dwarfing rootstocks (see pages 38–39) which fruit quickly and regularly. The training of these trees can provide an extra fascination and challenge to those with time to spend on it. Fruit trees may also be grown in pots. Soft fruit bushes like currants or gooseberries can be grown as specimen shrubs near the path (and therefore easily reached), but the bushes will have to be protected against birds. Perpetual-fruiting strawberries make ideal edging plants beside paths.

Ornamental plants offer endless variety. Cheerful, colourful annuals, especially those with scent like sweet peas, tobacco plants and petunias, look well in raised beds or pots but do need regular watering. Alpine and rock plants are perfect for the aged or infirm gardener. Grow in well-drained gritty soils in raised beds. There is no end to the fascination or choice and many are very low-maintenance indeed (see pages 28–29). For those who can afford it, the luxury of a small alpine or cold glasshouse is well worth considering.

Shrubs and perennials that provide low-growing ground-cover are also maintenance-free and reliable.

Fragrant plants and scented gardens seem especially appropriate for those with time to sit and breathe in the perfume, including the poor-sighted or blind. Scent may come from the flowers, often in the evening, or from the aromatic foliage, especially when lightly bruised. This table of a few labour-saving aromatic plants may help in the choice.

Fragrant plants

Name	Season of Flowering
Flowering Shrubs	
Chimonanthus praecox (Winter Sweet)	December-January
Viburnum carlesii	April
Osmanthus delavayi	April
Daphne 'Somerset'	May
Rosa rugosa types and many others	June-August
Philadelphus (Mock Orange)	June-July
Lavenders	June/August
Flowering Perennials, Annuals etc.	
Cheiranthus (Wallflower)	March-May
Hesperis (Sweet Rocket)	April-May
Dianthus (Pinks)	May-July
Lilies – especially the Madonna Lily, *Lilium candidum*, and *L. regale*	June-July
Phlox paniculata varieties	June-August
Nicotiana (Tobacco Plant)	June-October
Sweet peas	June-September

Plants with aromatic leaves

Herbs like rosemary, thyme, lavender, lemon balm, chamomile and camphor plants. Shrubs (to be kept in sheltered, protected places or in pots) like lemon verbena (*Lippia citriodora*), myrtle, bay and *Choisya ternata*.

4. Site and Soil Preparation

The soil is the basic material of the garden in which all plants normally grow (or do not grow in some cases!) and it is made up of a complex and fascinating blend of ingredients. The greater part is called the *mineral fraction,* the finer clays, sands or coarse gravels and stones that really give the soil such a variation of character; and then there is the highly important *organic humus* content made up from decayed plant or animal remains, leaves, root debris. The amount of this organic matter will determine the texture and water- and food-holding capacity of the soil. Finally there are the myriads of living organisms, so small as to be called micro-organisms; the bacteria, fungi and animals, harmful and beneficial, that also play an

important part in the life of the soil. We must not forget either the seeds, especially weed seeds, often present in huge quantities – up to 50,000 seeds for every square metre of soil in the top few centimetres.

So, the first thing even the most labour-saving gardener must have is a respect for this unique material called soil and a willingness to handle it carefully and to improve it, if necessary, by common sense and not necessarily by laborious means. The management of this complex and apparently inert 'dirt' is critical to the success of gardening, but often gardening books go overboard in their detailed instructions of how to cultivate or manage soil.

To dig or not to dig

Is it always necessary to dig soil, as invariably urged by so many of the manuals, or to drain or double-dig or trench or otherwise deeply disturb? The answer for the labour-saving gardener is, in most situations, no!

Digging is the inversion or breaking up of the upper layer of soil to incorporate organic matter, to reduce compaction and provide a deeper root-run for plants and let in more air and perhaps water. Vegetable food crops need this deeper worked, free-rooting soil but, for most ornamental gardening purposes, so much can be done by relatively shallow digging and the building up of a good organic layer on the surface. This will encourage earthworms and other soil organ-

isms. These will improve the structure of the deeper soil naturally.

There is a case for digging where the 'natural' soil has been devastated by building or engineering works, especially in a new garden on a housing estate where builders and contractors treat the soil (dirt to them!) in the most abominable manner. Lorries and equipment may have compacted the 'soil' or what is left of it and a thin film of imported top soil may cover a layer of rubble, flattened soil or rubbish. This layer needs breaking up with digging (or ploughing if the site is large) in order to begin building a new profile. Tools for soil cultivation are illustrated on page 58.

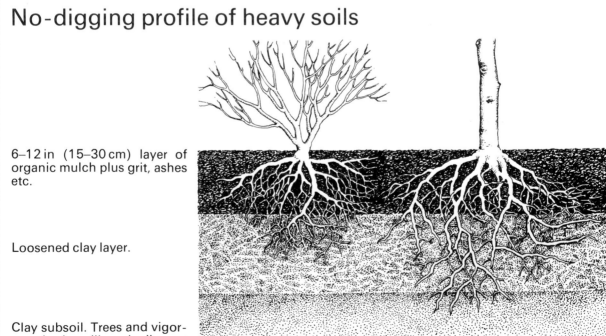

No-digging profile of heavy soils

6–12 in (15–30 cm) layer of organic mulch plus grit, ashes etc.

Loosened clay layer.

Clay subsoil. Trees and vigorous shrubs will gradually root into this layer.

A table of labour-saving soil management

Soil type	Characteristics	Management
Heavy soils, clays and silty loams	Very fine, closely packed particle sizes give wet, heavy soils, often badly drained in winter, drying out to a hard lumpy condition in summer. Lack 'open' gritty texture. May be acid or alkaline and often need plant foods.	Except for vegetables, and cut flowers, go for a 'no digging' approach and build up an organic layer by mulching and shallow forking-in of peat, compost, chopped straw, ashes, grit etc. Keep off in wet weather.
Light, sandy or 'gravelly' soils	Loose, light, open texture. Always free-draining so easily cultivated even in winter, but can become very dry in summer. Often quite acid and 'hungry', needing plenty of plant foods and organic matter. Often a low pH.	Easy to handle, so ideal for weeding and labour saving. To keep up fertility, they do need annual mulches, bark, sawdust, rotted manure and annual dressings of plant fertilizers. Water new plantings thoroughly until established.
Chalky and limestone (Calcareous soil)	Often shallow loams over the parent rock, free-draining and easy to work. They usually have high pH and are liable to deficiencies in iron and magnesium. Never dry out as much as sandy soils.	As above. Frequent mulches help conserve moisture and plant nutrients. Add additional iron or magnesium in the fertilizer if plants look anaemic. Avoid lime-hating plants, especially those in the heath family (Ericaceae).
Unclassified or disturbed and mixes of soils	A real mix-up of soils can be found on building sites, new estates etc., as already discussed. Rock-hard, compacted condition often with a variety of debris. Break up the pan and fork in organic matter. Pave or gravel bad places.	A slow, patient build-up of a new soil structure. Remove largest bricks, stones, old iron etc. Deep digging is a good thing and add rotted manure plus mulches and plant foods.

Soil Texture

The relative size of particles, magnified 80 times.

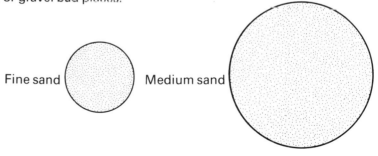

Clay o   Silt ◯   Fine sand   Medium sand

Soil pH

It is helpful to understand that most soils fall into three categories as regards the amount of lime or calcium present.

High pH soils which contain fair to large amounts of free calcium have a pH reading of 7.0 to 8.0.

Neutral soils contain less amounts of free calcium and usually have a reading of 6.0 to 7.0.

Acidic soils which have little or no calcium present or available to plants give a pH reading of 5.5 to 6.0 or even lower.

The pH scale is a means of measuring the hydrogen ions in the soil, which are in turn affected by the presence or absence of calcium.

Labour-saving gardeners are strongly advised to choose plants adapted to the average pH of the soil (testing kits are cheap and simple to use) rather than to try and alter this to suit particular groups of plants. Vegetable and fruit crops prefer a neutral or slightly alkaline soil, so lime may have to be added where soils are rather acid ('sour') to make them 'sweeter'.

5. Grass, Turf and Lawns

The lawn is usually the one common feature of most gardens, and a feature that can absorb as many hours of care and attention as its owners wish to devote to it. So much depends on the quality of lawn that is wanted and the uses it may be put to.

There is no doubt, of course, that unless maintained regularly, a lawn will soon change into a piece of grassland or meadow or a weedy neglected place. For labour saving then, we must see how it may be possible to save time and effort in the upkeep of lawns while still having an acceptable result.

Design

Perhaps we should first question whether a lawn is really necessary in the existing garden or in a new one to be planned. Can we dispense with it in favour of paving, gravel or the hard surfaces reviewed on pages 6–7? It would certainly save a good many hours of mowing over the years but then we must accept that for most gardens there is nothing quite like a lawn to look at and relax upon.

So we should study the proposed or existing size or shape of the lawn and see to what extent mowing in particular can be reduced or simplified. Too many small and awkwardly shaped pieces of grass can be tiresome to mow, apart from all the edges to cut. Use mowing strips as shown on page 7 and try and link larger areas of grass into pleasing, flowing shapes that give continuity of mowing with gentle curves the mower can follow. Turf over small beds that seem pointless and remove narrow grass paths that can be replaced easily by gravel or paving. Steep grass banks and slopes could in places be replaced by ground cover (see pages 30–31). Where there are extensive areas of mown grass, consider the possibility of converting some of these into attractive meadow gardens (see pages 60–61).

The type of grass

The fact that grass and lawns are found everywhere in gardens and countryside can cause an all too common lack of appreciation of the many different types of grasses and other plants that make up turf. It is this variation in species composition that can have such important effects on the character, wear and colour of a lawn, mowing frequency and drought resistance. Faster-growing types like the rye grasses (*Lolium*) or some of the meadow grasses (*Poa*) are hardwearing, but will need cutting much more often than the finer-leafed, denser and slower-growing fescues (*Festuca*) and bents (*Agrostis*). For labour-saving lawns, therefore, concentrate on the low-maintenance type and slower-growing strains summarised in the table opposite.

Their disadvantages are that they are not particularly hardwearing and cost more; so if these are important points, the rye and meadow grasses will have to be included in the mixture. These are available with the above included in varying proportions depending on the type of lawn wanted. A blend of tufted and creeping species gives the best close-knit sward.

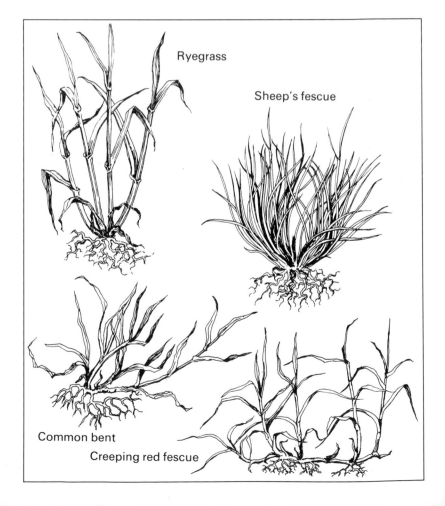

Ryegrass

Sheep's fescue

Common bent

Creeping red fescue

Grass type	Qualities	Sowing rate	Mowing height
Fescues			
Festuca rubra Red Fescue Creeping Fescue Chewing's Fescue	Fine leafed rhizomatous, for well drained, acid or alkaline soils. Drought-resistant. Many new strains.	¾ oz to the square yard (21 grams per square metre).	½–¾ in (12–18 mm).
Bent grasses			
Agrostis tenuis Brown Bent	Fine leafed, creeping and rhizomatous. Prefer acidic, poor, well drained soils. Many new strains.	¾ oz per square yard (21 grams per square metre).	½–¾ in (12–18 mm).

Establishing a lawn

You will certainly save time and effort later if you take the trouble to prepare and make a lawn carefully. The shape and size has already been referred to, but firm even surfaces are also crucial when it comes to mowing. Slopes and gentle contours can add interest to a lawn, but humps and hollows due to hasty preparation and levelling will be a nuisance.

Seeding is cheaper than turfing and you can prescribe a specific low-maintenance mixture, but there is the business of preparing a smooth, reasonably stone-free and firm seedbed. Turf can be laid at almost any time of the year but seeding is most successful between April and September.

An existing lawn of coarse grasses and weeds, provided it is firm and level, can be converted to an improved mixture by killing off the sward with a suitable herbicide and, after raking the surface of dead grass, overseeding with the new mixture.

Mowing

This is an essential job that cannot be avoided, usually meaning a weekly or fortnightly cut in the growing period but much less often in dry periods. Research has shown that leaving the mowings on the grass can produce a better sward, so only remove them if the swathe is very thick and long, usually in the flush growth periods, or if the lawn has not been mown for several weeks. Do not cut closer than ½ to ¾ in (12 to 18 mm). Close scalping does not save mowing frequencies but actually injures the grass roots and makes the grass more susceptible to drought. Types of mowers are discussed on pages 46–47.

Different mowing zones can also be created to add interesting effects and perhaps save maintenance. Here are the possibilities:

Close mown grass at a height of ¾ in (1.8 cm) will require 25–30 cuts per year.

Intermediate 'paddock-length' grass in informal gardens at a height of 2–4 in (5–10 cm) will require cutting 6–8 times a year.

Meadow or 'hay-length' will need mowing twice a year – see pages 60–61.

A spacious, well mown lawn with no complicated edges, and good ground-cover planting at the side. The cylinder mower gives the striped effect.

6. Planting

Planting, even for the most labour-saving among us, is probably the single most important treatment that you will give a plant in its new life in your garden. Planting really is worth a great deal of time and trouble to ensure healthy sustained growth later on and to avoid the possibility of failure. The old saying 'A penny for the plant, and a pound for the planting' is still very sound advice.

A good plant to start with

The first important step is to start with a good, healthy, well grown plant whether it be a seedling, perennial, shrub or tree. Be selective in the nursery and garden centre and look for well shaped, freely growing plants that have a look of well-being about them. Avoid stunted and straggly plants even if the price is much reduced. Where plants are available in containers, and so many are now, beware of pot- or container-grown shrubs and trees in particular, where roots may be curled up in a ball and which often fail to grow normally when planted out. Such plants can be deformed for life by their start in the nursery!

When to plant

Now that all kinds of garden plants are grown in containers in the nursery it is possible to plant out all the year round. Certainly with the less bulky, shallow-rooted subjects like shrubs, perennials and alpines, there may be a real advantage in planting out in the spring or early summer rather than in the winter; soil temperatures are higher, weather conditions are much more suitable for working outdoors and the plants often grow away immediately with no real check. For ornamental trees, larger shrubs and fruit trees and bushes, with more extensive root systems, planting open-ground nursery stocks in the dormant season between November and March is to be preferred. Late spring planting of this sort of stock into April, is risky, especially as the weather is normally dry then and frequent watering will be necessary.

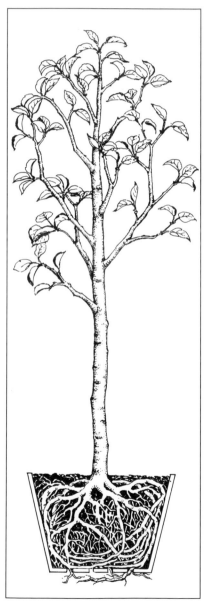

Don't buy badly grown or curly-rooted trees and shrubs that have been kept too long in containers. They are usually permanently disabled!

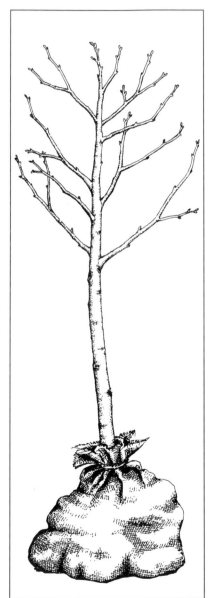

Plant trees and shrubs lifted from the open ground in the winter months. Be sure to get them into the ground as quickly as you can.

How to plant

The essentials are a well prepared pit or hole (for trees and shrubs especially) and then careful planting, treating the root systems with great respect, and following up with an after-planting service to help the plant become established in its new home.

1. Trim back very long roots.

2. Dig the pit wide and deep enough to take the roots comfortably.

3. Loosen the bottom of the pit, especially if the ground is very hard.

4. Add well rotted manure or peat to the soil around the roots to give the plant a good start.

5. Stake taller trees, but insert the stake before planting so as not to damage the roots.

6. Plant at the same depth as in the nursery.

7. Water well, and finish with a 2 in (5 cm) layer of mulch.

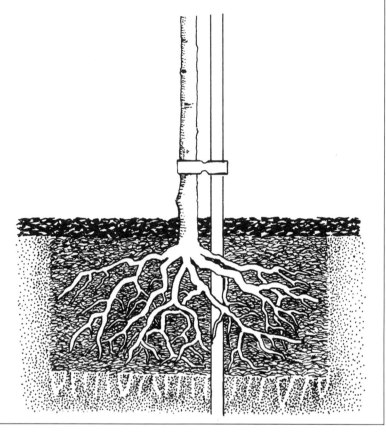

After-care

As a general rule if a plant has been well planted as shown and given a good soaking and mulching afterwards, no further watering should be necessary except in very dry spells. As fertilizer will have been added with the soil or mulch at planting, no more feeding is needed for at least a year, if then. The other essential job is keeping all weeds and grass away from the new plant. These compete severely in the first year or so, especially where trees are planted in grass. Weeding can be done by hand, or with a suitable chemical (see pages 48–49). Shallow-rooted herbaceous plants will benefit if you use peat in the soil at planting and add a mulch; these may need watering in very dry spells to get them established.

Protection

It is rather strange and an irritating fact that new plants arriving in a garden are often the target of wildlife like rabbits and birds. They seem to find them a tasty new addition to their diet and will nibble them for a time, or totally consume them, while leaving similar plants already in the garden untouched! It is usually in the first year of planting that most of the damage is done, and in this period some form of protection may be possible by using netting or special guards for trees and shrubs.

A spiral guard for protecting young trees.

7. Labour-saving Shrubs and Roses

Shrubs are naturally bushy or much-branched in habit, of different heights, shapes, growth rates, flower and leaf colours and suited to many different sites, sun or shade, wet or dry, sheltered or exposed and to acid or chalky soils. In a labour-saving shrub you must look particularly for the following:

1. A moderate to long life (10–20 years or more).
2. Hardiness and ability to withstand any bad weather in your area.
3. Relative freedom from pests and diseases.
4. Ability to live without regular attention, including pruning, for many years.
5. Slow or moderate growth if it is to live in a smaller garden or restricted space.

Types of labour-saving shrubs

BACKGROUND SHRUBS
Occasional light pruning. Some are good substitutes for hedges – with good foliage and some flowers or berries. Average height 6–11 ft (2–3.3m)

Cotoneaster x watereri – evergreen, red autumn berries.
Cotoneaster franchetii – evergreen, orange autumn berries.
Viburnum burkwoodii – evergreen, scented spring flowers (habit and flowers illustrated below).
Osmarea burkwoodii – evergreen, scented flowers in May.
Berberis darwinii – evergreen, yellow spring flowers.
Genista cinerea – yellow flowers in June, July.
Hydrangea villosa – pale lilac flowers in late summer.

SHRUBS FOR GENERAL USE
These can be placed in a mixed border or general planting scheme. Average height 3–6 ft (1–2 m).

Berberis thunbergii atropurpurea – purple leaves, autumn berries.
Camellia x williamsii hybrids – evergreen, pink, white, red flowers, need lime-free soil.
Cotoneaster salicifolius 'Autumn Fire' – evergreen, red berries.
Hypericum 'Hidcote' – evergreen, yellow flowers July–October (habit and flowers illustrated below).
Kolkwitzia amabalis – "Beauty Bush", pink flowers in May, June.
Prunus tenella – "Dwarf Russian Almond", bright pink flowers in April.
Mahonia japonica – evergreen, yellow winter flowers.
Escallonia 'Apple Blossom' – evergreen, pink and white summer flowers.

GROUND COVER SHRUBS
Once established after 3–4 years these are excellent for smothering weeds and covering banks and slopes, especially in shade or part shade. Clipping occasionally is the only real attention. Really labour saving. Height up to 1 ft (30 cm).

Cotoneaster salicifolius 'Repens' – evergreen, red autumn berries.
Hedera helix 'Hibernica' – "Irish Ivy", evergreen, large dark green leaves.
Cytisus x beanii – yellow flowers in May.
Vinca minor – "Periwinkle", evergreen, bright blue summer flowers (habit and flowers illustrated below).
Erica carnea 'Winter Beauty' – evergreen, pink flowers in winter.
Euonymus fortunei vegetus – evergreen, pink berries in autumn.
Potentilla arbuscula – yellow flowers summer and autumn.

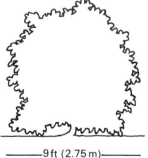

—9 ft (2.75 m)—

—5 ft (1.5 m)—

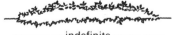

—— indefinite ——

Roses

Roses are really deciduous flowering shrubs. Many thousands of modern hybrid roses have been bred from wild or botanical roses, some of great antiquity and historical associations. These modern blends of garden roses are selected for large, brightly coloured flowers and a succession of display and plenty of vigorous shoots, which really only come from regular pruning and replacement of old wood with new, plus plenty of feeding and the incessant watch for an array of pests and diseases. The more attention you give them, therefore, the more you will be rewarded. But where do roses fit into the labour-saving garden where such attention may not be forthcoming? This is where *shrub* or the older *botanical* roses are very useful.

Shrub roses are usually classified into two groups:

Botanical or species roses

These have Latin or botanical names and grow wild in many temperate continents of the world. Those from Asia and Central Europe gave rise to the old 'Damask' and very fragrant cabbage roses and the red and white 'York and Lancaster' roses. Many of them make attractive long lived bushy shrubs, covered in sweetly scented white, pink or red flowers in June and July, and they need very little pruning or attention. Their main drawback is that many only have one rather short flowering period, but some produce attractive fruit or hips in the autumn.

Hybrid shrub roses

These are selected types or hybrids between the species roses and the hybrid tea or floribundas and others, and they often produce more flowers of brilliant colours, but rather less scent, over a longer period. The hybrid musk roses are good examples such as 'Penelope' or 'Buff Beauty'.

Rosa × *alba* 'Celestial' is a fine, healthy old shrub rose.

Pruning shrub roses

There are two sorts of occasional pruning you may have to deal with after a time. One is suckering. It is a nuisance that most shrub roses (like the modern bush roses) are all budded on to dog rose seedling rootstock, which tends to throw up suckers. These suckers have more leaflets on them than the bush roses and can usually be distinguished quite easily and cut or dug out at once, but with botanical or the older shrub roses, there can be quite a similarity between the actual variety and the sucker. Unless they are removed, however, they can often take over the whole bush which then reverts to the briar or 'dog rose' stock. Roses can be propagated on their own roots but rose growers still find the results more uniform and economic by budding.

The second pruning is of old or dead shoots and branches. After many years some shrub roses become too dense and overcrowded, and very old wood may die, so perhaps every 5–10 years a thorough thinning is a 'good thing' in late February or March. Old flowering shoots may also be removed with such hybrid types as 'Penelope' that do produce hips quite freely.

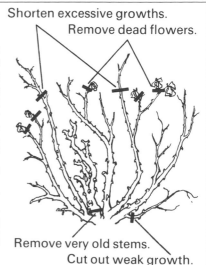

Shorten excessive growths.
Remove dead flowers.

Remove very old stems.
Cut out weak growth.

8. Trees for Small Gardens

Trees are the most dominant and permanent plants in the garden and can be used in many ways to give character and individuality and a feeling of permanence. They can also provide:
- Framework and background.
- Screening and shelter, especially from wind, noise and curious people.
- Shade, dense or dappled.
- Specimen effects and focal features.
- Colour – flowers, fruits, leaves, twigs and bark.
- Refuges for birds and animals.

From the labour-saving point of view, trees are fairly maintenance-free, if the *right kind* is planted in the *right place*. It is vital that you select and position trees correctly if you want them to be labour-saving and to give you long-term pleasure. Fast-growing, bulky trees like poplars or sycamores soon take up too much space, and shut out views and the light, and will need frequent topping or ugly pruning to keep them within bounds. The roots of some species like willows and poplars may affect drains, foundations and paths.

Go for slow-growing, shapely trees with attractive leaves, flowers, fruits or bark and twigs. Many have specific growth habits also that can be fitted into the design of the garden. A selection of trees for small gardens is given here. They have been chosen for their reliability, moderate growth rates and decorative value. They may take time to make any impression, but will be worth this in the long run. All those below are deciduous.

Trees with a columnar or fastigiate habit

Carpinus betulus 'Columnaris' A green-leafed, reliable hornbeam. Good autumn colours. 26 ft × 10 ft (8 m × 3 m).

Prunus × hillieri 'Spire' Upright, ornamental flowering cherry. Soft pink flowers in May. Autumn colour. Approximate size 26 ft × 10 ft (8 m × 3 m).

Sorbus aucuparia 'Fastigiata' Dark green leaves and red berries on this erect Mountain Ash. 26 ft × 13 ft (8 m × 4 m).

Trees with a weeping or pendulous habit

Prunus subhirtella 'Pendula Rosea' Early-flowering cherry, pale pink flowers. Good autumn colours. 13 ft × 10 ft (4 m × 3 m).

Sorbus aucuparia 'Fastigiata'

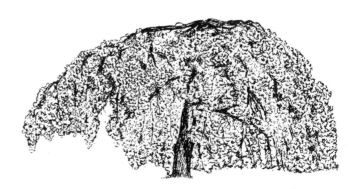

Prunus subhirtella 'Pendula Rosea'

Prunus × yedoensis 'Ivensii'   Snow-white cascades of scented cherry blossom in late March and April. Autumn colour. 10 ft × 10 ft (3 m × 3 m).
Pyrus salicifolia 'Pendula'   Weeping Silver Pear. Silvery grey, willow-like leaves. Small white flowers. 13 ft × 10 ft (4 m × 3 m).
Salix purpurea 'Pendula'   Dainty, weeping, purple-stemmed willow. Purple winter twigs. 10 ft × 6½ ft (3 m × 2 m).

Trees with a rounded or traditional shape

Acer griseum   The slow-growing Paper Bark Maple with mahogany-brown peeling bark, three-lobed leaves and good autumn colour. 16½ ft × 10 ft (5 m × 3 m).
Betula papyrifera   Paper Bark Birch. Brilliant white trunk and branches. 19½ ft × 10 ft (6 m × 3 m).
Crataegus prunifolia   A plum-leafed hawthorn with shiny leaves, large red fruit and brilliant autumn colour. Approximate size 16½ ft × 10 ft (5 m × 3 m).
Robinia pseudoacacia 'Frisia'   The brilliant golden-leafed False Acacia. Prefers shelter and associates well with grey or purple themes. 19½ ft × 13 ft (6 m × 4 m).

Trees with a vase or funnel shape

Malus hupehensis   Very reliable flowering crab apple. Pink/white flowers, small red fruit. 26 ft × 19½ ft (8 m × 6 m).
Prunus 'Accolade'   Dainty ascending habit. Fringed pink petals, cherry flowers in April/May. Good autumn colours. 19½ ft × 13 ft (6 m × 4 m).

Evergreen trees are much less numerous for small gardens, being either too large, or most often forming bulky, bushy shrubs. However, there are a number of attractive hollies with variegated leaves and berries that are very adaptable and hardy and also laurels, bay trees (for milder areas) and of course many different conifers (see pages 26–27).

Pruning or surgery work

If trees do get too large, or are damaged or shed branches, some sort of pruning and surgery work is obviously inevitable. Always cut branches back to the collar at the base and do not leave snags. Painting sawn cuts is now not recommended. Thinning the crown of heavily branched trees can also let in light and reduce the risk of wind damage. For tall trees, call in the advice or services of a reputable tree specialist.

Robinia pseudoacacia 'Frisia'

Prunus 'Accolade'

9. Herbaceous Perennials and Bulbs

Herbaceous perennials and bulbs really are worth a place in the labour-saving garden. So many are quite easy to grow and establish without too much trouble and their colourful flowers and the decorative softness and texture of the foliage do make pleasing seasonal contrasts to the more permanent, subdued and sometimes sombre shrubs, conifers and ground cover.

Herbaceous perennials do not have to be grown in the more labour-demanding old-style herbaceous borders with all that staking and continual lifting and dividing. Such plants can be used in different ways for reasonably low-maintenance and attractive effects.

Space will not allow the detailed listing of the many possible good plants that could be recommended for garden planting, but here is a basic summary of some reliable, fairly permanent and reasonably easy-care ones.

Good flowers and foliage

Achillea millefolium 'Cerise Queen'   Bright cerise flowers in summer. $2\frac{1}{2}$ ft (75 cm).
Bergenia purpurascens   Evergreen with rosy-purple flowers in spring. 9 in (23 cm).
Epimedium   Semi-evergreen. Pink, yellow or white flowers in spring. Grow in shade. 9 in (23 cm).
Euphorbia characias   Evergreen. Yellow-green flowers in late spring. Very drought-tolerant. 3 ft (90 cm).
Geranium macrorrhizum and other varieties.   White or pink flowers late spring. Good ground-cover in shade. $1–1\frac{1}{2}$ ft (30–45 cm).
Helleborus corsicus   Icy-green flowers late winter to early spring. Evergreen. 2 ft (60 cm).
Hemerocallis (Day Lilies)   Shades of pink, red, yellow in summer. For sun or shade, damp sites. 2–3 ft (60–90 cm).
Iris sibirica   Blue, white, violet or plum flowers in summer. Moist site. 3 ft (90 cm).
Peonies   White, pink, red flowers, single or double. Long-lived plants for sun or part shade. $1\frac{1}{2}–3$ ft (45–90 cm).

Easy, colourful flowers in attractive clumps

Aster × frikartii   Lavender-blue Michaelmas Daisy. Flowers summer to autumn. 3 ft (90 cm).
Coreopsis verticillata   Yellow daisy flowers all summer. $1\frac{1}{2}–2$ ft (45–60 cm).
Doronicum   Yellow daisies in spring. For damp shade. $1\frac{1}{2}$ ft (45 cm).
Geranium endressii   Ground-cover with pink flowers all summer. 1 ft (30 cm).
Phlox paniculata   Many colours in late summer. Grow in part shade. Fragrant. Up to 3 ft (90 cm).
Salvia × superba   Purple spikes in summer. Grow in sun. 3 ft (90 cm).
Stachys macrantha   Showy pinkish-mauve spikes in summer. $1\frac{1}{2}$ ft (45 cm).

Bold, statuesque plants

These need more space but thrive on neglect for years, often in quite shady places, heavy soils and those awkward spots.
Acanthus spinosus   Glossy, cut leaves; mauve and white flowers. 3–4 ft (90–120 cm).
Aruncus sylvester (syn. **A. dioicus**)   Flowers in creamy plumes in summer. 4 ft (1.2 m).
Crambe cordifolia   Huge sprays of starry white flowers in summer. 4–6 ft (1.2–1.8 m).
Crocosmia masonorum   Orange-red, red or yellow flowers above sword-like leaves in late summer. Moist site. 3 ft (90 cm).
Hosta species and cultivars.   Ground-cover for shady, damp sites. 2–3 ft (60–90 cm).
Miscanthus saccariflorus (syn. **M. floridulus**)   Very tall ornamental grass. 8 ft (2.4 m). *Miscanthus sinensis* is also very good.
Phlomis russelliana (syn. **P. viscosa**, syn. **samia**)   Yellow whorled flowers in summer. 3 ft (90 cm).

Maintenance of perennials

As the majority of these plants die away in the winter they will need cutting back eventually, but to save time and trouble leave all this until the early spring after frosts. Cut off all dead growth and trim back the evergreen types which benefit anyway from an annual tidy-up to prevent them getting leggy; this applies especially to many silver and grey-leafed plants. Give a light dressing of general fertilizer and then mulch with a 2 in (5 cm) layer of shredded bark or leaf mould etc.

Normally most of the plants suggested will thrive for five to six years before they require lifting or dividing. This is only necessary when their growth weakens and they begin to decay in the middle of the clumps. Now is the time to lift them, preferably in early spring. Split off the younger outer growth and replant it, discarding the old material. Flag irises are best divided after flowering, usually in July.

Stachys macrantha

Daffodils and Erythronium dens-canis

Bulbs

There are many beautiful bulbs, from miniature alpines to tall woodland flowers, but here we are also concerned with those that will come up and flower year after year. Choose dependable kinds, place them where they will be happy and *don't disturb*. Plant them usually in late summer, autumn or early winter – even after Christmas if you keep them dry and cool. A general rule is to plant no deeper than twice the height of the bulb, except for tulips which prefer deeper planting. All need good drainage. After flowering, leave the foliage uncut to build up next year's bulbs – so don't mow grass containing bulbs until ten weeks after the flowers are over.

Early spring
Grow these on rock banks etc. or through thin ground-cover. All except the cyclamen can be naturalised in thin turf.
Crocus chrysanthus   Beautiful flowers – white, yellow, blue, mauve. Grow in sun.
Crocus tomasinianus   The earliest of all crocuses. Shades of mauve.
Cyclamen coum   Delicate white or pink flowers for sun or half shade.
Galanthus (Snowdrop)   Sun or half shade. Always a welcome sign of spring.
Narcissus – early species.   Many miniature daffodils like *N. bulbocodium* appear early.

Spring
In mixed borders through thin ground-cover. Naturalise in thin turf, open woodland and at shrubbery edges; hedge bases, in rock gardens and in raised beds. The fritillary is especially suitable for mixed borders.
Anemone appenina   White or blue starry flowers. 6 in (15 cm).
Anemone blanda   White, blue and pink. Similar to above. 4 in (10 cm).
Chionodoxa   Clusters of blue or pink flowers on 6 in (15 cm) stem.
Erythronium dens-canis   Rose-purple flowers with reflexed petals. 6 in (15 cm).
Fritillaria imperialis   Yellow or orange-red bells hanging from a central stem up to 3 ft (90 cm) high.
Narcissus   Plant drifts of daffodils in turf for a labour-saving spring display.
Scilla   Shades of blue and mauve clusters of stars. 6–8 in (15–20 cm).
Tulipa species, especially *T. fosteriana* types with their huge flowers ranging from white, yellow to scarlet. 1–2 ft (30–60 cm).

Summer
Grow in the mixed border, in sun or light shade.
Allium siculum   Beautiful bell flowers, banded russet and blue. 2 ft (60 cm).
Gladiolus byzantinus   A lovely hardy gladiolus with bright magenta flowers. 2½ ft (75 cm).
Lilies, especially *L. martagon* and *L. regale*, which are both easy to grow.

Late summer/autumn
Grow in 'wild' parts; but the amaryllis and crinum are best grown at the foot of hot, sunny walls.
Amaryllis belladonna   Pale pink trumpet flowers. 2–2½ ft (60–75 cm).
Colchicum   Pink, lilac and white forms which naturalise well. 6 in (15 cm).
Crinum × powellii   A striking flower with pink or white lily trumpets. 2–3 ft (60–90 cm).
Crocus speciosus   Vigorous and free-flowering. Lilac shades. 6 in (15 cm).
Cyclamen hederifolium   White or pink dancing flowers. Good in half shade. 4–6 in (10–15 cm).

10. Hedges and Living Screens

There are many good reasons why most gardens should find a place for some form of hedge or living screen. For those who want to have a minimal-labour garden, the answer to their problems can be found here, even with hedges. Here are good reasons for a hedge or screen:
  – For marking boundaries or defining areas.
  – Protection from intruders, dogs and (most important) shelter from winds and draughts.
  – To create a secluded and private sanctuary by visual screening.
  – To make decorative living walls.

Choosing a hedge

All sorts of woody plants, trees, conifers and shrubs can be turned into hedges by repeated pruning or clipping, but a labour-saving hedge should really have the following points in its favour:
  – Easy to establish and grow.
  – Limited clipping frequency, no more than once a year preferably.
  – Dense, twiggy growth and attractive habit.
  – Compact, non-invasive and non-greedy root systems.
  – A long, effective life.
Clipped hedges give that neat, formal, ordered boundary or enclosure and they may be curving, in straight lines and even intricate patterns as in a maze. To keep maintenance to a minimum choose the slower-growing kinds, that keep well furnished to their bases. The height will vary considerably depending on the purpose, but it should also be assessed in relation to the time it takes to cut the hedge. Here are some good labour-saving hedges.

Type	Main characteristics	No. of cuts per year	Ideal height
Deciduous hedges			
Beech (*Fagus*)	Purple or green-leafed; persistent brown winter leaves; good on chalky soils.	One (in winter)	6–9 ft (1.8–2.7 m)
Field maple (*Acer campestre*)	Quick to establish. Easy on all soils. Green-leafed.	One (in winter)	4–6 ft (1.2–1.8 m)
Hornbeam (*Carpinus*)	Quick to establish. Easy on all soils. Green-leafed.	One (in winter)	4–6 ft (1.2–1.8 m)
Evergreen hedges			
Berberis julianae	Spiny, long-leafed barrier. Really anti-vandal. Scented yellow flowers.	One (in May)	4–6 ft (1.2–1.8 m)
Holly (*Ilex*)	Shiny, prickly-leafed, long-lived. Green or variegated. Any soils. Stands salt spray.	One (in March)	6–10 ft (1.8–3 m)
Laurel (*Prunus laurocerasus*)	Rather large, shiny leaves. Needs space. Good in towns.	One (in March) Use secateurs	6–10 ft (1.8–3 m)
Thuya plicata (Western Red Cedar)	Glossy scented cypress-like foliage. Stays green at base. Superior to Lawson Cypress.	One (February to March)	6–9 ft (1.8–2.7 m)
Yew (*Taxus baccata*)	The best architectural hedge. Dark green. Likes chalky soils. Leaves poisonous to animals.	One (August to September)	4–9 ft (1.2–2.7 m)

The very common *Lonicera nitida* and privet have been left out of this list, chiefly because they need quite frequent clipping, usually in the summer too, when there is so much else to be done. Privet is also a very greedy hedge, as is Leyland Cypress because of its excessively fast growth and maintenance requirements.

    Another maintenance point is that the higher the hedges (nice for shelter and seclusion) the longer it takes to cut them, a job that requires usually steps or ladders. A very convenient height for most garden hedges is 4 to 6 ft (1.2 to 1.8 m).

Living screens

You can make screens or backgrounds of unclipped or lightly pruned, dense-growing shrubs or conifers by choosing them for their foliage contrast or flowers or fruits. They give a less formal appearance to the garden but will need more space in which to grow. Use evergreen shrubs like *Viburnum tinus*, × *Osmarea* 'Burkwoodii', laurels, hollies and on acid soils rhododendrons. Choose also deciduous shrub roses, forsythias, *Kolkwitzia amabilis*, *Viburnum opulus* (Guelder Rose) and a number of bushy conifers (see pages 26–27).

Dwarf hedges

There are quite a number of dense, low-growing shrubs that make neat hedges for edging paths, borders or vegetable or herb gardens. Lavender, santolina, rosemary and Burnet roses are good for these hedges, needing usually one or two clippings a year, one after flowering and one in early spring. Box hedges are also attractive, but will need two to three clips during the summer.

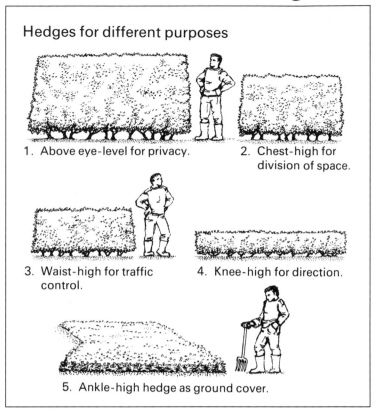

Hedges for different purposes

1. Above eye-level for privacy.
2. Chest-high for division of space.
3. Waist-high for traffic control.
4. Knee-high for direction.
5. Ankle-high hedge as ground cover.

Planting hedges

Time and disappointment can be saved if hedges are carefully planted following the procedures shown on pages 14–15. Start with well-rooted, bushy plants and a well-prepared site. Plant them at these distances apart: for most taller deciduous hedges 1½ to 2 ft (45–60 cm); for evergreens 2½ to 3 ft (75–90 cm); and for dwarf hedges 1 ft (30 cm) apart. Only clip the sides of the taller growing hedges in the earlier years and then the tops when the required height has been reached. Mulch well and feed annually, on poor soils particularly.

Clipping

There are now a number of speedy, powered hedge cutters that can save hours of work in comparison with hand shears, if used properly. Hiring one for a long, tall hedge may be a sensible alternative to buying one, as it will inevitably spend much of its time idle in the garden shed. Shears are still excellent for dwarf or for a shorter length of hedge and should be kept well oiled and sharpened. Also choose a good reliable make.

Hedge renewal

Many hedges eventually become old, gaunt and scraggy (like humans alas!) but some can be rejuvenated (unlike humans) by a drastic cutting back to the old trunk or even the ground and by feeding and mulching to encourage new growth and a new hedge. Yew, holly, beech, hornbeam, laurel and rhododendron can be treated in this way but not cypresses or thuya. These last two should be removed when really old and you must start again. If you attempt to cut them back you run a high risk of killing the hedge.

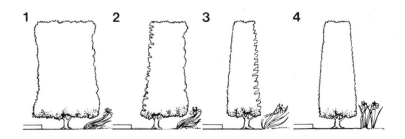

1. Overgrown hedge. 2. One side cut hard back.
3. The other side cut back one year later.
4. The slim rejuvenated hedge.

11. Climbers and Wall Plants

Climbers and wall plants can be one of the most labour-intensive groups of plants in a garden, involving considerable pruning and tying up as well as some spraying and feeding. Yet they are important and necessary for enlivening walls, clothing fences and trellis work and they often provide a feeling of luxuriance which is difficult to achieve with any other form of planting.

So a rational approach is necessary here, since there are a number of labour-saving climbing and wall plants we can choose. Here are some guidelines for doing this.

Choosing, climbing and wall plants

1. Concentrate on those that really are self-clinging and twining, if not from the start, at least when established.

2. Forget about, or be very selective with climbing roses; they are lovely and colourful but really need quite a lot of attention throughout the year.

3. Choose climbers that don't engulf the garden and the neighbours, too, before you have time to sit on the terrace! There are less vigorous kinds that only need an overall pruning in late spring or after flowering.

4. Put up adequate supports, wires, pergolas, trellis, tripods etc. before you plant. This saves much time in the long run.

5. As many climbing plants are often on walls of buildings, soils beneath may be dry and rubbly, so plant carefully and give annual mulches and a slow-release fertilizer dressing in February or March.

6. Don't be afraid to mix several climbers together for a tapestry effect and a longer season of colour, provided they are all of about the same vigour.

Sensitive use of different climbers to decorate but not smother the attractive flint and brick wall.

Golden hop and purple clematis – a companionship which remains spectacular for a long time.

Self-clinging climbers

Plant	Habit/site	Pruning etc.
Hedera (Ivy) *H. helix* and varieties	For shade or sun, on walls, fences etc. Many varieties with gold, grey or variegated leaves.	Clip over occasionally when too luxuriant or growing behind gutters etc.
Hydrangea petiolaris (Climbing Hydrangea)	For cold, shady walls or tree stumps etc. White flowers in June.	May need some help to make it cling to start with. No regular maintenance unless too bulky. Clip or prune in winter.
Parthenocissus henryana	Fine-lobed, green, bronze and white leaves. Loves shade.	Sucker pads cling determinedly. Clip back to allotted spaces in spring.
P. quinquefolia (Virginia Creeper)	Fine-fingered, glossy leaves. Brilliant autumn colour. Good up big walls, trees etc.	Give plenty of space. Loves deep shade. Restrain by pruning any time.
P. tricuspidata (Boston Ivy)	The familiar vine-leafed curtains of green, blazing to scarlet in autumn. Needs lots of room. For shade or sun.	Very vigorous so restrict by pruning any time. Stands really hard cutting back.
Trachelospermum asiaticum	Warm, sheltered sunny walls. Sweetly-scented, white flowers in July. Evergreen.	Clip when exceeding allotted space after flowering.

Twining or twisting climbers

Plant	Features, habit, etc.	Pruning etc.
Clematis	So many to choose from but concentrate on the following: *C. macropetala*, *C. jackmanii*, *C. viticella* and hybrids and *C. montana* and other species types; they are long-lived and have a long flowering season.	For part shade or sunshine. Prune back lightly in early spring until they exceed the room available then hard prune annually in late winter, early spring. Wilt disease can cause sudden deaths.
Humulus lupulus 'Aureus' (Golden Hop)	Nice for scrambling through other creepers, evergreen shrubs or up a tripod or pergola. Mix with clematis. Soft golden leaves.	Prune back hard every spring.
Jasminum officinale (Summer Jasmine)	Ferny leaves, scented white flowers in summer. Warm walls or trellis.	Prune early spring back to previous year's wood. Frost damage in cold areas.
Lonicera (Honeysuckle)	Choose scented free-flower types, like 'Americana' and 'Serotina'. Good for cooler walls.	Aphids may be a problem on very dry warm walls. Prune in winter to old wood.
Solanum crispum (Climbing Potato)	Blue-mauve clusters of flowers July to September. Warm walls, fences etc. Likes chalky soils.	Occasional trimming in spring.
Vitis vinifera (Grapevine)	Choose ornamental foliage types like 'Brant' and 'Purpurea'. Shade or sun. Good leafy cover for pergolas etc.	Prune back hard in late winter or early spring.

Roses

There are many free-flowering, attractive, climbing or rambling roses for fixing against walls, over posts or pergolas but they seldom have a natural twining habit and do need a fair amount of training and attention. Some reliable and easily grown ones are 'Zephirine Drouhin', which is thornless, pink and scented; 'New Dawn', pale pink; 'Sanders White', which has an overpowering fragrance; 'Lawrence Johnston', scented, lemon-yellow; and 'Francis Lester', single, pale pink and scent of apple blossom.

Thuya plicata

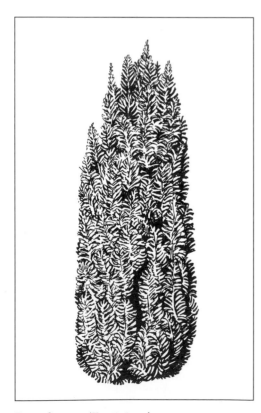

Taxus baccata 'Fastigiata'

12. Conifers

The conifers are a remarkable group of woody, mostly evergreen plants distributed over much of the world and characterised by their stiff, rather symmetrical habit of growth, their resinous needle or scale-like leaves and their cones or, occasionally, berries. They include some of the tallest trees in the world (Giant Redwoods) and some of the smallest (very dwarf types). They are also near perfect, labour-saving plants, being relatively slow-growing, very adaptable and accommodating. They are obtainable in a variety of shapes, textures and foliage colours. Careful selection is nevertheless important, depending on the character of the garden and the space available, since some are quite vigorous and will eventually reach a large and dominant size.

Conifers for boundaries

Look for the relatively slower-growing, bushy varieties of Lawson Cypress (*Chamaecyparis lawsoniana*), making dense walls of pendulous branchlets in a range of foliage colours – gold, bright green, blue-grey and variegated. *Thuya plicata*, the Western Red Cedar, has a fine gold-variegated variety called 'Zebrina'. All these can be topped at 10–15 ft (3–4.5 m) and lightly trimmed occasionally in spring. The bushier pines are also very attractive especially on light sandy soils – *Pinus sylvestris* 'Nana', *Pinus cembra* and *Pinus parviflora* – and for larger gardens there are the Scots Pine, Austrian Pine and the Larches. These are also fine for copses, backgrounds and shaded areas.

Columnar types as specimens

Height after ten years approximately 10–15 ft (3–4.5 m). There are many distinctive, slow-growing, upright conifers that can give a statuesque quality and vertical accent in most garden schemes. All these recommended will grow in most well-drained soils in sun or part-shade.

Chamaecyparis lawsoniana 'Columnaris' Grey feathery column.
Chamaecyparis lawsoniana 'Ellwoodii' Light, grey-blue, slow-growing.
C.l. 'Fletcheri' Similar to the above.
Juniperus communis 'Hibernica' (Irish Juniper) Very slow-growing, with grey, prickly foliage.
Juniperus virginiana 'Sky Rocket' Narrow, fast-growing; cypress-like habit; steel-grey-blue foliage.
Taxus baccata 'Fastigiata' (Irish Yew) Dark green, bulky column. Very slow-growing and permanent. There is also a good golden form.

All these columnar types may occasionally become misshapen by snow or wind or old age and a band or two of green, plastic-coated wire will keep them neatly corseted and trim.

Round 'bun-shaped' conifers

Height after ten years approximately 6–8 ft (1.8–2.4 m).
Chamaecyparis pisifera 'Nana'.
Chamaecyparis pisifera 'Boulevard' Feathery, silvery grey.
Thuya 'Rheingold' Yellow green in summer turning to orange gold in winter.

Slow-growing, spreading conifers

Spread after ten years approximately 8–15 ft (2.4–4.5 m).

Juniperus sabina tamariscifolia   Fresh green, aromatic mats. Excellent in dry and shady places.

Juniperus × media 'Pfitzerana'   Larger growing for dry banks and difficult sites; very reliable.

Specimen trees

Up to 30–40 ft in twenty years (9–12 m).

For the larger garden or where there is room for one or more feature trees as single specimens or small groups, conifers have the advantage of looking attractive at any time of the year, but may take a number of years to mature and outgrow perhaps eventually their living space. Do not be afraid, therefore, of planting some potentially big conifers, since you or your successors in the garden can enjoy their increasing beauty for twenty to thirty years or more before they may become a headache.

Many prefer acidic soils. Larches (*Larix*) are beautiful deciduous trees with fresh green leaves and pendulous branches. There are some attractive pines, few being better than our native Scots Pine. Blue Spruces need moister acidic soils, but the pagoda-shaped Serbian Spruce (*Picea omorika*) should be more widely grown. Also lovely and graceful are the Western Hemlocks (*Tsuga heterophylla*). A visit to the pinetum at the R.H.S. Gardens, Wisley will give you good ideas for many more.

These conifers are essentially labour-saving, needing little pruning or feeding for many years.

Chamaecyparis pisifera 'Nana'

Planting

Most conifers have a fairly restricted fibrous root system, seldom invasive or damaging but needing care at the planting stage. They are now usually grown in containers so that the root ball is not disturbed at planting. Use peat in the planting hole and water well. Keep grass and weeds away for several years until established. Enemies of dwarf conifers are dogs using them as urinal 'signalling posts', causing a scorching or browning effect.

Pruning

Never cut most conifers really hard since they normally cannot regenerate from old wood. Exceptions are yew and Californian Redwood. For the majority, if really old, or scraggy and brown, dig up and start again.

Juniperus × media 'Pfitzerana'

Dwarf conifers

There are so many of these available now – dwarf, prostrate, slow-growing species or varieties, representing most of the groups and associating very well with alpines, rock plants, heathers and dwarf shrubs. Provided they are not used to excess, they are really an ideal component of the easy-care garden, for they are remarkably maintenance-free (no real pruning), they are evergreen and bear foliage in a range of colours from grey, blue, various greens through to gold. They may live for very many years provided they do not get too dry or choked by weeds or other invasive plants. They do appreciate more neutral soils and plenty of mulching.

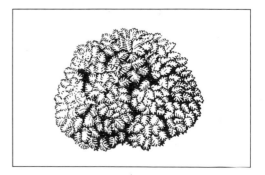

Picea abies 'Little Gem'

13. Alpines and Rock Plants

Botanically speaking true alpines are those dwarf, compact plants that are adapted to growing in the high, mountainous regions of the world, especially the Alps of Europe and temperate latitudes. Rock plants cover a rather broader category including any dwarf or spreading plants that naturally prefer to grow amongst stones, rocks or dry places. Both groups of plants therefore share the ability to survive in poor, dry, stony soils in full exposure and have a general dislike of deep shade or soggy soils. Such good-tempered, thrifty plants are therefore well suited in so many ways to the labour-saving garden. Being of modest size, often spreading, and with brightly coloured flowers, they are really ideal for small gardens and limited spaces and the variety available is astonishing. There are also so many ways of growing them in gardens today, as we shall see; in fact, the traditional rock garden or rockery, attractive though it can be, is not really the best place for growing such plants, on account of the maintenance involved.

Choice of plants is the first and most important decision. Go to a good alpine plant nursery or alpine show to get to know the many colourful easier ones to start with, avoiding the rather more tricky and specialist high alpines. Typical plants are to be found in the groups of saxifrages, and amongst rock phlox, campanulas, dianthus, helianthemums, sedums, sempervivums and many others.

The raised bed or dry terrace wall

A raised bed or dry terrace wall can be an ideal place for these plants, especially where there are sloping sites or where space is limited. There are all sorts of possibilities, but the general idea is to build a raised bed some 18–24 in (45–60 cm) above the path or grass level, using stone blocks, brick or treated timber (old railway sleepers are ideal) for the walls. The advantage of stones or blocks is that trailing plants can be encouraged to grow in the joints. For special acid-loving plants, peat blocks may also be used. It is essential to have free-draining soils, so put in a layer of rubble, crushed bricks or coarse gravel and then fill up the bed to just above the wall level, when firmed,

with a gritty mixture made up of approximately 2 parts chippings, 1 part coarse sand, 1 part good loam (must be weed-free) and 1 part horticultural peat. After planting, cover the bed with a layer of 1–2 in (2.5–5 cm) of fine chippings – a neat mulch that also conserves moisture. You can vary the contours on the surface of the bed with a few well-placed rocks, but the range of plants will also create different heights and shapes. These may include many alpines and rock plants, dwarf bulbs, dwarf conifers and slow-growing shrubs. A narrow, dry-stone or brick wall may also be used to edge a terrace, and coping stones can be placed at intervals to provide somewhere to sit.

Old or new paving slabs, crazy paving or bricks laid with joints on sand can be a pleasing and very effective way of growing carpeting rock plants or cushion-forming plants, especially if the paved area has only occasional casual use.

Old stone troughs are scarce and expensive these days but splendid for small alpines and miniature plants. Glazed sinks are more often to be found and these can be treated with a peat and cement mixture to simulate stone and then planted up.

Rock outcrops

There is much to be said for making one or more carefully sited and constructed outcrops of rock perhaps in place of a rock garden, which is of course another way of growing alpines, though one which is all too often used as a place for bedding out. You will need a natural slope for the best effect, and a few pieces of an attractive natural stone such as water-worn limestone, ragstone or sandstone. After grouping these in as natural a stratum as possible, fill in between the stones with a gritty compost and plant with a few of the thrifty rock plants already mentioned. Use a few large pieces of stone rather than a mound of small pieces of stone, which does look unsatisfactory. Such a well-built feature will last four years with the minimum of attention.

Maintenance

Once they have settled down in their various homes, alpines and rock plants need very little attention. Clipping after flowering or in the spring, weed control (this is essential) and some protection against slugs are the main jobs. Top dressing with chippings every two to three years and occasional feeding are all they require. Some are shorter-lived than others but those suggested can be very reliable indeed.

Some reliable cushion plants

Aethionema Pink-flowered, grey-leafed semi-shrub; for gravel.
Dianthus alpinus (Alpine pinks) Many hybrids; for walls, paving.
Erinus alpinus Pink or white flowers; for steps, walls, paving.
Saxifraga aizoon Silvery cushions, white flowers; for paving, walls, gravel.
Sempervivums (House Leeks) For dry places; very tolerant.

Some reliable spreading plants

Acaena Green or silvery sheets. For paving etc. A good ground-cover.
Antennaria dioica Grey mats, pink or white flowers. For very dry places.
Campanula carpatica and many other blue or white bell-flowered campanulas. Trailing and spreading in walls, paving, gravel.
Geranium sanguineum Free-flowering Cranesbill. For banks, slopes and walls.
Hypericum olympicum Yellow flowers: grows in shade.
Phlox subulata and **douglasii** Mauve, red, pink sheets of flowers on soft, mossy carpets. For semi-shade.
Thymus drucei (Creeping Thyme) Aromatic-leafed carpet for paving and gravel.

This gently sloping site has been landscaped with gravel and some stones. Crazy paving slabs are stepped to form a path which gives easy access to a wide area. The plants include many that are densely weed-smothering in growth, such as colourful and spreading campanulas, low-growing hardy geraniums, carpeting rock plants and evergreen conifers, and these reduce the amount of upkeep needed in such an area. The gravel, which is easy to keep weed-free, serves the same purpose as a mulch, keeping the plants' roots cool and moist, yet perfect drainage is ensured by the slope of a site such as this.

14. Ground-cover

Ground-cover has become a fashionable catch phrase in modern gardening, usually associated with labour saving and low-maintenance gardens. Ground-cover plants are usually those of low, spreading habit, shrubs or herbaceous, that will knit together to form an effective dense carpet, smothering the weeds and covering the soil.

What are good ground-cover plants? Not all ground-cover plants are all that they are supposed to be and if you are to select effective candidates, you should look for the following qualities when choosing such plants:

  – Ease of establishment.
  – Rapid and consistent growth after planting.
  – Reliability and low maintenance.
  – Attractive appearance for most of the year.
  – General availability.

Using ground-cover

Preparation must be really thorough if these plants are to be expected to smother weeds. The ground must be cleared of vigorous perennial weeds like couch, ground-elder or buttercup and preferably kept fallow with regular hoeing or herbicides to reduce annual weeds.

Ground-cover plants are only appropriate in certain places. A whole garden covered with such plants would look monotonous and boring. They are useful on steep shaded banks, under trees, between specimen shrubs, in wild gardens, in areas as a contrast to mown grass and to fill odd spaces between paths, beds

Ground-cover for shade

E = evergreen; F = fast cover; Fl = colourful flowers; S = slow-growing; Sh = shrub.
Measurements = height × planting distance.

Ajuga reptans (Bugle)   Fl, 3 × 12 in (7.5 × 30 cm)
Asarum europaeum   E, F, 6 × 12 in (15 × 30 cm)
Bergenia   E, Fl, S, 12 × 24 in (30 × 60 cm)
Cotoneaster salicifolius 'Repens'   E, F, Sh, 6 × 36 in (15 × 90 cm)
Epimedium species   E (some), 15 × 36 in (38 × 90 cm)
Euonymus radicans   E, Sh, 6 × 24 in (15 × 60 cm)
Euphorbia robbiae   E, 12 × 24 in (30 × 60 cm)
Galeobdolon luteum variegatum   F, Fl, 6 × 36 in (15 × 90 cm)
Geranium macrorrhizum   F, Fl, 9 × 36 in (23 × 90cm)
Hedera helix varieties (Ivy)   E, Sh, S, 6 × 36 in (15 × 90 cm)
Hypericum calycinum   Fl, Sh, 15 × 36 in (38 × 90 cm)
Juniperus conferta   E, F, Sh, 6 × 36 in (15 × 90 cm) (Also suitable for sun.)
Juniperus horizontalis   E, Sh, 10 × 48 in (25 × 120 cm)
Lamium maculatum   E, Fl, 4 × 24 in (10 × 60 cm)
Lonicera pileata   E, Sh, 24 × 36 in (60 × 90 cm)
Rubus tricolor   E, F, 12 × 48 in (30 × 120 cm)
Taxus baccata repens   E, S, Sh, 18 × 36 in (45 × 90 cm)
Vinca minor   E, Fl, Sh, 9 × 24 in (23 × 60 cm)
Viola cucullata   F, Fl, 6 × 24 in (15 × 60 cm)
Viola labradorica   F, Fl, 6 × 12 in (15 × 30 cm)

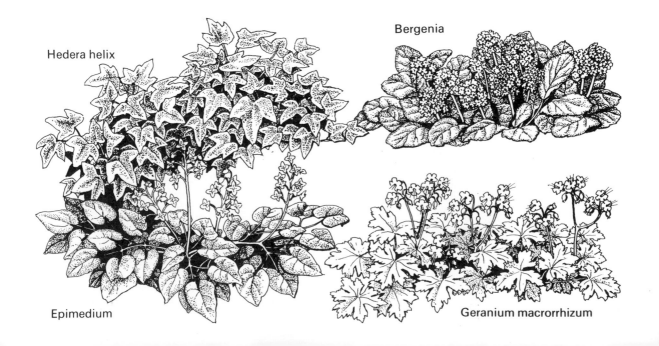

Hedera helix

Bergenia

Epimedium

Geranium macrorrhizum

or buildings which might otherwise become weedy corners.

There are hundreds of possible ground-cover plants that might be used, since most plants in some way cover the ground, but one should be guided by the qualities already listed, the character of the garden, the intended places to be planted, whether shaded or hot and sunny, the type of soil and the rate of cover needed.

Not all of the best ground-cover plants are evergreen.

Maintenance of ground-cover

To keep ground-cover effective involves some care, albeit minimal. Here are the essential jobs:
- Remove any weeds as soon as possible, especially in the first two to three years before the plants have closed ranks.
- Clip over and tidy in the spring where necessary, especially the less shrubby types like hardy geraniums and dianthus or clip these after flowering.
- Replace dead or very old plants.
- With the slower-growing types like ivies and some heaths and conifers, use a mulch to encourage growth. In fact all ground-cover plants appreciate mulch from the start.
- Watch out for the over-invasive sorts that may overwhelm borders and take you over. Give these more room and restrain them by clipping or even treading on them or banish them from the garden!

Try different associations of tapestry effects with ground-cover and increase the colour by underplanting with suitable bulbs. There is plenty of scope here (see the photograph on page 5).

Ground-cover for sun

E = evergreen; F = fast cover; Fl = colourful flowers; S = slow-growing; Sh = shrub. Measurements = height × planting distance.

Acaena microphylla   F, 2 × 15 in (5 × 38 cm)
Bergenia   E, Fl, S, 12 × 24 in (30 × 60 cm)
Calluna vulgaris varieties (Ling)   E, Fl, Sh, acid soils, 12 × 15 in (30 × 38 cm)
Cerastium tomentosum   E, F, 3 × 36 in (7.5 × 90 cm)
Dianthus hybrids (Pinks)   E, Fl, 6 × 12 in (15 × 30 cm)
Erica species (Heaths)   E, Fl, Sh, 12 × 15 in (30 × 33 cm)
Genista hispanica   E, Fl, Sh, 24 × 30 in (60 × 75 cm)
Genista lydia   E, F, Fl, Sh, 24 × 30 in (60 × 75 cm)
Geranium endressii   F, Fl, 9 × 36 in (23 × 90 cm)
Hebe 'Pagei'   E, Fl, Sh, S, 12 × 24 in (30 × 60 cm)
Hebe rakaensis   E, Fl, Sh, S, 15 × 24 in (38 × 60 cm)
Helianthemum varieties   E, F, Fl, Sh, 9 × 24 in (23 × 60 cm)
Juniperus procumbens   E, F, Sh, 12 × 36 in (30 × 90 cm)
Juniperus sabina tamariscifolia   E, Sh, 15 × 24 in (38 × 60 cm)
Lavandula dwarf forms   E, Fl, Sh, 12 × 12 in (30 × 30 cm)
Nepeta mussinii   F, Fl, 12 × 24 in (30 × 60 cm)
Polygonum affine   F, Fl, 9 × 24 in (23 × 60 cm)
Rosa paulii   F, Fl, Sh, 15 × 36 in (38 × 90 cm)
Sedum species and varieties   E, Fl, 6–12 × 15–18 in (15–30 × 38–45 cm)

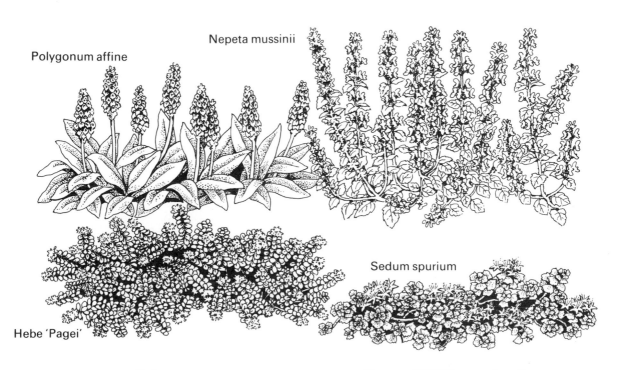

Polygonum affine

Nepeta mussinii

Sedum spurium

Hebe 'Pagei'

16. Herbs and Vegetables

We are verging on the labour-intensive garden once we start on the vegetables and to a lesser extent herbs, so this section is very selective and intended as a guide to the easier and more rewarding plants that may be fitted into the labour-saving garden. First some definitions:

HERBS   These are aromatic shrubs or perennials, ornamental or used primarily for flavouring and seasoning in food and of easy and reliable growth.

VEGETABLES   In this context, choose primarily the more easily grown types and salad vegetables that can be fitted into small areas and that do produce crops with a modest work input.

Herbs

The essential thing to remember when growing herbs is that most of them like an open, very well-drained position. The aromatic shrubby types like rosemary, sage and thyme originate from Mediterranean regions where they grow on dry, warm, stony hillsides, often baked in the long summer and these are the sort of conditions to aim for in the garden. Within reason the warmer and drier, more rubbly and even chalky the soils, the longer-lived will be these types. The leafier perennial types like mint and parsley prefer deeper, moister soils and will even grow in the shade.

For the labour-saving garden, the secret is to decide how and where to grow these herbs so that they are handy to use and not too much of a chore to look after.

The following shrub types can be used as edgings, or low hedges in dry borders around a sunny terrace, or in raised beds. Don't go for a herb garden unless you are sold on such a feature. The maintenance can be quite a headache.

Reliable shrubby and bushy types These include sage (green, golden or purple), rosemary, thyme, winter savory, lavender, origanum, marjoram, southernwood and curry plant (*Helichrysum*). All these are very drought-tolerant and easily renewed from cuttings, and if clipped hard after flowering or in the spring, should last for years.

Herbaceous perennial types These could include the various mints, lemon balm, the umbellifers like fennel, angelica and dill and the various sorrels, tansy etc. Some of these are tall and vigorous and mints can be invasive. They will all grow in quite shady places in odd corners and perhaps even in a wild garden, so perhaps this is a clue as to where to put them. They can also be used in mixed borders, cut back in spring. Keep perennial weeds out of the clumps. Fennel, chives and parsley are best renewed from seed every few years but fennel will usually seed itself freely all over the garden if allowed. The bronze-leafed form is very decorative.

A raised herb bed containing small shrubby types which will survive dry conditions and give a valuable supply of aromatic leaves or flowers without much attention.

Vegetables

For the labour-saving garden one must be very selective and not be tempted into buying all sorts of packets of seeds in the spring in a spurt of exuberance, and either not sowing them because time or land runs out or despairing after sowing, because only half the seeds come up and the eventual crop was not worth the effort. If you are near a good local pick-your-own enterprise you can get fresh green stuff from the local market or shop. In such a case it is scarcely worthwhile finding a place for vegetables when there are so many other ornamental things you can grow.

Lettuces You can either go for a continuous succession of lettuce leaves rather than hearts by growing the cos varieties at close spacings, new leaves coming from the old stumps; or you can choose the newer butterhead or crisp head varieties which will give nice hearted lettuce from May to August. Buy plants in the packs now available in most plant centres ready for planting out, rather than sowing seeds. Late summer lettuce are a problem, so avoid them.

Brassicas Avoid Brussels sprouts and cauliflowers which demand more cultivation, but you could find room for a few rows or groups of such tasty and welcome types as purple-sprouting broccoli, curly kale or spring cabbage. These are planted out in the late summer or early autumn and mature in the spring. The main problem is pigeons who will devastate them in the winter, as will rabbits, so if you have either of these visitors and have no time to protect the plants, forget about growing them. Calabrese are similar to purple-sprouting broccoli but are planted out in early summer for autumn cropping. Runner beans are attractive, colourful climbing plants, easy to grow and free of pests provided they do not have to compete for water with other plants in the cropping period. Mulch well and water in very dry spells. Plant out in late May.

Potatoes Even a few plants in rows of the early salad types are well worth a trial. The flavour and pleasure of your own potatoes is quite marvellous and a few rows of these types are well worth the effort. Main crops are hardly worth the bother.

Spinach Spinach is also very easy and so generous with its endless succession of leaves. Sow a short row as edging or in a border and the results are always gratifying.

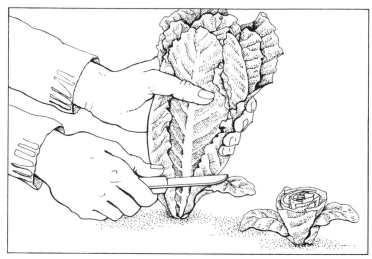
Cut-and-come-again lettuce gives two crops.

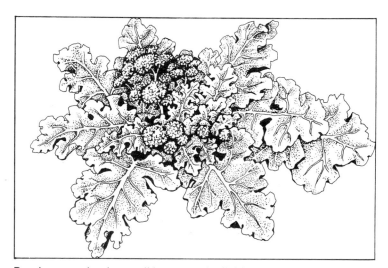
Purple-sprouting broccoli is easy and reliable.

Curly kale provides delicious leaves in the winter months.

17. Pools and Aquatic Plants

Ponds and water gardening are objects of fascination in the garden. Apart from the water itself, whether still or moving, there are the many attractive plants and the additional interest of the fish and pond life. Once made and established, pools can be surprisingly easy to maintain but, as with so many constructed garden features, the secret of success lies in the thoroughness of the planning and preparation.

Here are some important points to think about before making a start:

1. Siting: Pools should be sited in the sunniest possible place and certainly away from overhanging trees or branches. Heavy shade and leaf-fall upset the healthy life of the pool and there is the chore of removing leaves in the autumn.

2. Design: Simple, realistic shapes, fitting into the pattern of the garden, are usually the most effective to build, to look at and to look after.

3. Construction: Here too lies the secret of labour saving for the years ahead. Money and time are well spent on the materials and the making of the pool. Cheap, quick short cuts will be regretted later.

4. Choice of plants: Very critical indeed, once the pond is made. Its size and design may determine the sort of plants you can grow, whether at the margins or in the water.

What style of pool?

This will depend on the size and space available, the money, and the tastes of the owner. For less complicated building and simplicity of upkeep later, go for a formal shape, round, or rectangular and edged with paving; or choose one of those garish and instant fibreglass affairs that can be dropped into a suitable pit albeit at very considerable expense. Don't be tempted into Japanese- or Swiss-inspired creations of rocks, streams, waterfalls or water gardens if you are really looking for the minimum of work or trouble. All great fun but not for those reading this book.

Here are some of the various options you can choose when making a pool together with an approximate estimate of the life.

Material	Estimated life
Concrete	20 years – the best.
Fibreglass	10 years – but instant!
Butyl rubber liners	20 years – quick, reliable method.
Polythene liners	2–5 years – risk of damage.

Depth and water balance

One often sees a 'natural' pond in the countryside that seems to stay clear and healthy-looking without any apparent water-flow or aeration. This is all to do with the so-called 'balance' of the pool – a balance between the many inhabitants of the watery environment, the plants, the fish and other pond life; and all this is closely connected with the site and the depth of water. If everything is right, the pond will remain clear and healthy for a long time. Water depth is important here. Average ponds should be 15–24 in (37–60 cm). A newly filled pond, especially in full sun, will usually go very green to the dismay of its proud owner, but this is normally caused by rapid growth of green-celled algae in the freshly filled water. After a time when the new plants, fish, snails and other livestock all get to work, the pool should clear. As a general rule, it is far easier to get these clear, balanced conditions in larger pools. Small pools are difficult. Pools over 40 sq ft (3.75 sq m) will often remain clear, while very small pools may stay cloudy. If all else fails, chemicals like Algizin can be added to the water to clear the algae.

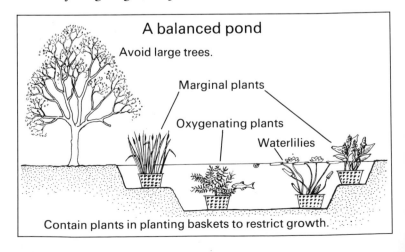

A balanced pond

Avoid large trees.

Marginal plants

Oxygenating plants

Waterlilies

Contain plants in planting baskets to restrict growth.

The plants

The right choice of plants is the secret of the labour-saving pool. Here is a selection of some reliable species, classified into the different types found in or around water.

Oxygenating plants   These can fill the watery space of the pool very quickly if they get out of hand, but they are important for helping to aerate or oxygenate the water and to provide refuge for fish etc. Whether they are floating or rooted in crates, pots or in the pond bed, allow about one plant per 2 sq ft (0.18 sq m) of water. The following are not so vigorous:

> *Ceratophyllum demersum* (Hornwort)
> *Eleocharis acicularis* (Hair Grass)
> *Fontinalis antipyretica* (Willow Moss)
> *Hottonia palustris* (Water Violet)
> *Hydrocharis morsus-ranae* (Frogbit)

Waterlilies   These are exotic, exciting and usually the most desirable plants in a pool. There are varieties to suit different sizes of pool but in very small pools they can quickly outgrow their welcome. Here is a brief selection of lilies, all of which belong to the family *Nymphaea*.

> For small pools 6–12 in (15–30 cm) deep.
> *Nymphaea pygmaea* 'Alba' – white.
> *N. pygmaea* 'Helvola' – yellow.
> *N. laydekeri* 'Purpurata' – wine red.

> For medium pools 12–18 in (30–45 cm) deep.
> *N. amabilis* – salmon pink.
> *N. 'Escarboucle'* – bright red.
> *N. marliacea* 'Chromatella' – yellow.
> *N. odorata alba* – white.

Marginal plants   These always need their 'feet' in moist ground, or shallow water. They can be aggressive but make an attractive informal edge to a pool.

> *Butomus umbellatus* (Flowering Rush)
> *Caltha palustris* (Kingcup)
> *Iris kaempferi* (Japanese Iris)
> *Mimulus luteus* (Monkey Musk)
> *Sagittaria sagittifolia* (Arrowhead)
> *Scirpus tabernaemontani* 'Zebrinus' (Zebra Rush)
> *Typha minima* (Dwarf Reedmace or Bulrush)

Nymphaea 'Escarboucle'

A summary of pool maintenance

Regular
– Keep water levels topped up in dry weather.
– Remove debris, leaves etc. especially in autumn. Covering with a nylon net can save the tedious hand-pulling of dead leaves out of cold water.
– Restrain oxygenating plants by hand-pulling.

Every three to five years
– Drain pond if necessary and lift and divide overgrown clumps of lilies, rushes etc. Spring is a good time to do this.

An informal pool luxuriantly planted with reliable aquatic plants.

18. Fruit Trees and Bushes

We are concerned here with a specialized group of trees and shrubs that have been selected over a long period of time for their main characteristic, that of producing good fruit. But they can also be decorative and there are dwarf forms that fit nicely into small gardens or compact spaces. Being woody plants, though, they can occupy the ground for a considerable time, so the first question to ask is whether there is a place for fruit trees or bushes at all in your labour-saving garden. They are by no means trouble-free and the fruit has to be picked. It really is pointless occupying valuable space with such plants when it might be easier to go to the nearest 'pick your own' enterprise and pay that little extra to someone else whose business it is to grow fruit properly.

If the decision is made to grow some fruit, provided it does not demand a great deal of time or effort, there are ways and means of reducing the input considerably. Here are the main categories of fruit suggested:

TREE FRUITS – Apples, pears, plums and cherries.
BUSH FRUITS – Black and red currants and gooseberries.
CANE FRUITS – Raspberries and blackberries.

Tree fruits

Apples   Popular and remarkably adaptable, apples have been grown in gardens for centuries, usually as elaborately trained trees, or in orchards. Today we can get apples grafted on to rootstocks that control the size and the cropping and the time taken to produce the first apples. Here are two possible systems of growing apples in the labour-saving garden:

1. As ornamental specimen trees.   In blossom and fruit they compare very well with ornamental flowering cherries and crab apples and can look very decorative as a lawn tree or in small orchards. Choose a variety on a semi-vigorous rootstock like MM11 and go for a cultivar like 'Worcester' or 'Sunset' or 'Discovery' that fruits fairly regularly without too much spraying or attention. Plant as half-standard trees and prune lightly to produce shapely trees in the early years.

2. As dwarf screens, hedges or fences.   Start with apples on a dwarfing rootstock such as M27 or M9 and plant about 1 m apart, as shown in the illustration. Pollination and pests and disease-control should not be too much of a worry if one does not regard the fruit as a major part of the household diet. Both systems of growing are best in clean ground with a mulch around the trees for at least the first two to three years. Grassing down can follow after that, especially for the orchard trees.

Plums and damsons   Although delicious to eat ripe from the tree, plums have a doubtful place in the labour-saving garden. They tend to flower rather early when the frosts are about and bullfinches can wipe out the flower buds. They also crop rather erratically from one season to another and are somewhat prone to aphids. They prefer deeper fertile soils. One place to grow them is against a wall if one is prepared to train them accordingly.

Damsons are much more suitable for the larger garden as specimen trees or in small groups where they can be left alone to look after themselves and produce fruit, perhaps rather intermittently over the years. They can be used for shelter belts too, and are fairly attractive trees.

Modern dwarfing rootstocks enable you to grow apples as bushes or hedges, making pruning and picking more manageable.

Cherries and pears   It may be worth thinking about growing cherries in the smaller garden now that there are newer dwarfing rootstocks like Colt and Pixie. Suitable varieties are 'Stella', which is self-fertile and produces sweet black cherries in late July; 'Waterloo' crops late June and can cross-pollinate with 'Van' (mid-July); or 'Early Rivers' (mid-late June) to cross pollinate with 'Bigarreau Schrecken' (late June).

As regards pears, I would forget them for the labour-saving garden.

Bush fruits

Black and **red currants** and **gooseberries** are fairly easy to grow in a variety of soils and places, even in quite deep shade, but sadly the main problem is caused by our feathered friends, the birds, who will constantly devastate crops when they are ripe. So protection is a must unless you happen to live in an area where birds are scarce. Protect them not only at fruiting time but also in late winter and early spring when bullfinches and perhaps blue tits can strip the buds off the dormant bare branches. A fruit cage is the only answer if the investment is considered worthwhile, but you may be able to buy quite a lot of pick-your-own soft fruits locally before you can recover the cost of the fruit cage, so perhaps other forms of bird deterrent can be tried, such as the new 'humming wires'.

Cane fruits

Raspberries are the most worthwhile of these. In my experience, an unprotected crop is less likely to be devastated by birds, since they cannot land easily on the upright canes. To grow them well, follow the guidelines here:

1. Start with good, clean, fertile ground.
2. Erect a structure of poles and wires for support; this is essential and if well done will last 10–20 years.
3. Buy healthy canes of a good cropping variety like 'Malling Jewel', 'Malling Enterprise', 'Glen Clova' or 'Admiral'.
4. Keep weed-free and mulch in late winter with a good layer of rotted straw plus a dressing of a balanced fertilizer. Winter weeds can be killed with a suitable herbicide such as paraquat.
5. Tie in canes as they grow. After fruiting the old canes will die away and these can be cut out in late autumn or early winter. Remember that raspberries are produced on a renewal system of canes every year. All this apparent work is usually well rewarded and, in fact, a good row of raspberries grown in this way may last for many years. If the raspberries start to look stunted and yellow after a number of years this is a sign to remove the canes and start again.

A line of raspberry canes requires some work initially, but once established can fruit well for years.

Strawberries I recommend growing perpetual-fruiting types or alpine strawberries as an edging to borders or in the vegetable area. These will fruit right through the summer and children particularly love them; they are small and sweet and delicious. Main crop types are really not for the labour-saving garden.

Rhubarb Whether this is a fruit or a vegetable does not really matter, but it is extremely easy to grow and quite free of any real upkeep needs apart from mulching, weeding and feeding occasionally. It will grow quite well in shady places and will last for years and years without much attention.

19. Labour Saving under Glass

Is there really a place for glasshouses, greenhouses and the like in minimal care gardens? Perhaps not, since growing plants successfully under glass can mean a fair amount of tender loving care and there are so many different sorts of plants that can be grown. There is also nothing worse than a sad, neglected and starving collection of plants in a badly maintained glasshouse.

So we must compromise here and assume that there is a place for some kind of glass structure; and of course in buying a property one may acquire a glasshouse and it is rather a hasty and unnecessary decision to knock it down or remove it before seeing what can be done to grow something in it.

What sort of glasshouse?

There is a bewildering range of makes, types and materials on the market at the moment and, if one is thinking of buying a glasshouse in our context, one must look for something simple, strong and easy to maintain. Aluminium or Western Red Cedar are both possible materials and, if the cost can be justified, think seriously of a lean-to structure placed on the south or south-west wall of your house. It can make a delightful extra garden-type room, it will benefit from the warmth of your house and, probably best of all, the reluctant gardener has not got to go for a long walk to the bottom of the garden to water or look after his plants; they are right under his nose and there to be enjoyed, perhaps while taking breakfast or reading the paper.

A sunny lean-to conservatory can be more labour-saving and easier to enjoy than a separate glasshouse.

What to grow?

We must assume the glasshouse will be unheated since, once you heat a house, you will be ensnared into growing all sorts of plants that you will probably not be able to look after. You can use your house for growing plants from seeds (see page 42) and also for growing plants permanently or semi-permanently in the house.

You can try edible crops in a cold glasshouse such as lettuces for winter or spring, followed by peppers, tomatoes and cucumbers in the summer. Grow all these on the floor of the house in growing bags or pots. Growing bags are usually of plastic, are 40 in (1 m) long, 15 in (38 cm) wide by 5 in (12.5 cm) deep and contain sufficient compost specially formulated to give immediate early growth; additional feeds follow to sustain a crop throughout the growing season. The growing medium is usually peat based, and these bags are economic to use, very easy to place in a glasshouse, on soil or hard surfaces, and are usually free of pests and diseases. It is very important to really soak the bag before planting, and never allow it to get too dry. One bag will need over $2\frac{1}{2}$ gallons (11 litres) of water to moisten it. Crops like tomatoes, peppers, cucumbers and melons and aubergines are ideal in growing bags, and strawberries also.

If you want more decorative plants you will have to remember that winter frosts may be the limiting factor, unless you have a lean-to house which will probably be more frost-free. Mediterranean plants like oleanders, citrus, jasmine and acacias, which are types for the cool conservatory, can be grown in pots and are very decorative. If you have benches or staging and are perhaps more elderly, alpines and rock plants love cold house conditions and are fairly easy to maintain. Herbs are also easy in cold glasshouses.

Pests and diseases may be a problem, since the comfortable environment you are creating in the glasshouse will attract various creatures like scale, mealy bug, aphids and red spider. There are some useful systemic insecticides to be used against these pests (see page 52), but do be careful about using them in living rooms.

Watering can be made more automatic these days to reduce labour with some quite sophisticated systems on the market. Three fairly simple systems that can be used in a glasshouse are illustrated on page 55.

Jasminum polyanthum – this tender, fragrant and vigorous climber must be trained to supports.

20. Easy Ways to Sow and Propagate

Propagation, or the multiplication of plants, is a fascinating business, whether you sow seeds or increase plants by vegetative cuttings or other means, but to succeed one must follow certain rules. This usually means a fair amount of care and attention at critical stages and may therefore be unsuited to the easy-care gardener. There are, nevertheless, some techniques that do simplify the rules and take the fussiness out of the propagation mystique, yet enable you to get some encouraging results and end up, one hopes, with more plants than you started with!

Seed sowing

There are basically two systems depending on the sort of plants you want to grow and the facilities available; sowing seeds under glass and sowing seeds outdoors. If you do have an unheated glasshouse there are certainly plenty of seeds one can sow in spring; but restraint is essential because it is not the sowing that takes the time but the handling of the seedlings afterwards and the watering, followed by the pricking out and the potting on, followed by the planting out in the garden afterwards. So choose things you want to grow and look after later, whether they are herbs and salad crops, parsley and thyme or annuals that if started early will come into flower sooner; cosmos, nicotiana, impatiens etc. All these seeds are best sown in small pots or segmented trays from which they can be planted out direct later in the spring. Tree and shrub seeds can be treated differently by sowing them in a gritty compost in pots, covering the compost with grit and standing the pots outside in a sheltered, shady place and perhaps watering them occasionally. You may have to protect them from birds or mice by netting them.

Sowing seeds directly outside is normal for vegetables but annuals can also be sown like this in a well prepared crumbly soil. Wait until the first weed seeds are coming up in the garden before you sow; this is an indication that the soil temperatures are about right for seed germination. In fact weeds, slugs and cats are the worst enemies of direct seed sowing outside so you may wish to forget this method or take necessary remedial steps.

1. Sowing seed into a seed tray. This stage can be avoided by sowing direct into a compartment-tray, shown below, or into the open ground if you wait until it is warm enough.

2. Pricking out seedlings into a compartment-tray for growing on.

3. The small plants are pushed out of the compartment tray and planted outside.

Cuttings

The propagation of plants by cutting can be rather tricky for most labour-saving gardeners, for it usually requires glass or polythene or frames and depends on a knowledge of the best time and best way to make the cuttings. However, there are some simple forms that we can think of for the labour-saving garden. If you have a glasshouse or lean-to house, cuttings of evergreen shrubs, sub-shrubs like lavenders, rosemary and even some of the woody house plants can be inserted direct into pots in a sandy soil mixture, covered in polythene and stood in the glasshouse or lean-to house. Provided you look at them from time to time and ventilate them occasionally you may get results this way. It is also possible to root a number of cuttings directly outside in the garden by taking what are known as hardwood cuttings. Choose a sheltered site and well drained soil and choose such deciduous plants as the ornamental poplars, willows, and some shrubs including, particularly, rambling, climbing and ornamental roses. In October or November take 10–12 in (25–30 cm) lengths from the newest growth of these plants (about the thickness of a pencil), make a slot with a spade 4–5 in (10–12 cm) deep, put a little sand in the bottom of the slot and push in your cuttings so they are about 3–4 in (7.5–10 cm) apart, firm well and with a bit of luck they will root during the following spring and summer. Smaller cuttings 4–6 in (10–15 cm) in length of such useful plants as lavender, rosemary, sage and pinks can also be rooted in shallow trenches in sheltered place. This costs nothing and is an interesting way of producing plants.

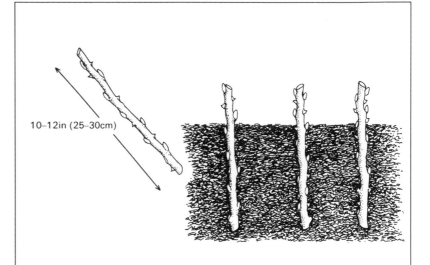

10–12in (25–30cm)

Hard wood cuttings taken from dormant, leafless trees and shrubs like willow, poplar, roses, black currants etc.

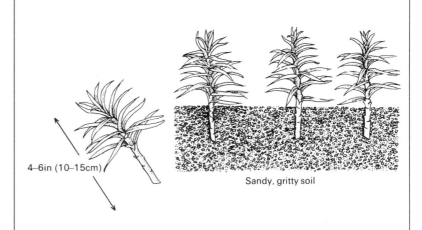

4–6in (10–15cm)

Sandy, gritty soil

Cuttings from evergreen shrubs like lavender, sage, pinks etc.

Division

The easiest way to multiply certain plants like herbaceous perennials (the non-woody types) is by dividing up clumps or rootstocks in autumn and early spring. Keep the younger healthy growths and plant immediately. Those plants that produce runners or rooted layers can also be increased by simply breaking up the plantlets and planting them out in moist weather.

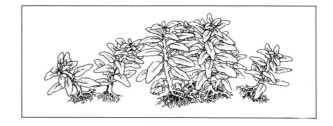

21. Pots, Tubs and Containers

There are now so many different sorts and sizes of containers on the market for plant growing and plant displays, ranging from the more classical terracotta urns and pots to the very contemporary concrete or plastic vases and bowls. The same variety is to be found among the different sorts of plants that can be grown in these containers, ranging from colourful temporary displays of short-term annuals, to the more permanent trees and shrubs that may last for years in the same pot or tub. Visitors to the great formal gardens of France may recall the array of tubs outside the orangeries, growing oranges and lemons, some of which are very old indeed.

A labour-saving approach

However, what must be the guiding principle in this chapter is the importance of labour saving in growing plants in containers, and in some respects, this is a contradiction in terms. Once a plant has been taken out of its mother earth and placed in a container, it is almost totally dependent on its owner for all its needs, for water, nutrients and possible pest and disease control. So a reduced-maintenance approach must be to grow the sort of plants that will get by with as little attention as possible, and to choose the sort of containers that will help in this respect.

Easy-maintenance planting in containers

1. Use the largest container you can afford or accommodate, perhaps simple half-barrels or wooden tubs; large containers have greater soil- and water-holding capacity. Depth is also important.

Fuchsias are one of the best plants for pots – colourful and easy to maintain.

A pot (unseen) enlivens a dark corner.

An unusual but floriferous container!

2. When you have decorative floral displays in containers, place them in part-shade to reduce dessication, and where they are handy for watering or where signs are immediately noticeable. Petunias, impatiens and nicotianas will all flower well in containers in shade.

3. Select more permanent types of plant. The range is large and there is great scope for trying out different associations of plants here. The photographs show the sort of thing you could try. For really low maintenance here are a few:

Alpines and succulents like sedums, sempervivums and also some saxifrages. They will last for years in quite shallow sinks without watering.

Conifers, especially the dwarf or slow-growing kinds, or others that will assume a bonsai-like habit – even though potentially large trees. The secret here is to give them just enough water and not to stand them in hot, dry places. The larger the container, the larger the specimen.

Some good evergreen shrubs like bay or box trees or, if on calcareous soils, selected, acid-loving rhododendrons (very low water needs), camellias or azaleas. Again stand the tubs in shaded patios or courtyards for low maintenance and long life.

4. Choose the right sort of soil or compost mix for the plant and the container. Loam-less peat composts are good for acid-loving shrubs and conifers, and many other plants, but they are inclined to dry out if not correctly watered. The compost does not show drought, being naturally dark in colour, so a drooping plant is the first sign of this. Therefore, allow a generous watering space by not filling the container too full; or use more of the John Innes soil-based compost to the approximate formula 7 parts soil (good loam if obtainable), 3 parts peat and 2 parts gritty sand, plus fertilizer. One can make up one's own mixture like this, but do not use plain garden soil without some peat and sand. Drainage is also advisable in the form of crocks, stones or rubble in the bottom of large containers.

5.   Feeding. For the longer-term plants like trees and shrubs in containers an annual or occasional feed with a liquid or soluble fertilizer is a good thing, as this feeding can compensate to a large extent for the limited size of the container and the plant's root ball. Re-potting into larger containers must reach a limit or final size and, as bonsai growers have shown, it is surprising how small a container can be used for an ancient tree.

22. Lawn Mowers and Grass Cutters

Lawns are the most regularly maintained features of most gardens and the average regularly close-mown lawns will need about 30 cuts throughout the growing season, which usually means one cut a week between March and October. The *width* of the mower and therefore the *cutting width* makes a great difference to the time taken to mow a lawn. Changing the height of cut may also mean mowing the grass less often.

All manner of aids and techniques are available today for lawn maintenance, with over 200 different sorts of mowers apart from the more traditional hand grass-cutting tools and the invaluable brush cutters or strimmers (see picture). Power mowers and brush cutters will help to save labour in the larger sized garden but don't forget that, thanks to recent research and grass breeding work, it is now possible to choose hard wearing and slower growing seed mixtures for the lawn that will need cutting less frequently. The labour-saving gardener may also adopt a more tolerant attitude to moss and weeds in lawns which have the effect of reducing grass growth by competition and which, after all, are green for most of the year (see pages 12–13).

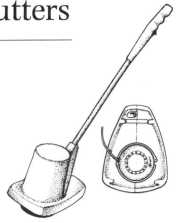

A small strimmer. The nylon cord shown underneath whirls round to trim grass around trees.

Cylinder mowers

Cylinder mowers, or reel mowers, may be hand or power driven and are the best machines to give the nicest finish to a lawn. Power-driven cylinder mowers are quite reliable and safe, of moderate petrol consumption and capable of living to a ripe old age if carefully used. Remember that the number of cutting blades on the reel will determine the quality of cut (the more blades the better the cut) but that these blades are easily damaged by stones or metallic objects. Cylinder mowers are not as versatile as rotary mowers. They pick up grass more easily (boxing off) and give a striped effect to lawns, but are not as good as rotaries with very long grass, or in wet weather and on borders and slopes. The petrol-driven models of both sorts are heavier and more robust than their electrically powered counterparts.

Rotary mowers

Are tough, adaptable and versatile, usually noisier than cylinders, use more petrol and are not really capable of cutting grass to the quality finish or closeness of the cylinders. They tend to produce a more spongy turf. Their high-revving blades are potentially more dangerous – watch your toes – and the hover types need sensible handling, especially on slopes. Rotaries are very versatile with all lengths of grass in wet weather and on steep banks and slopes. Grass collection is less necessary as they macerate the grass. Their useful life is usually shorter than the cylinders, but they have a comparatively simple cutting mechanism with less likelihood of damage or faults than the cylinders. The electric types (battery or mains) have less guts than the petrol models, and are handy for small lawns.

1.   2.   3.

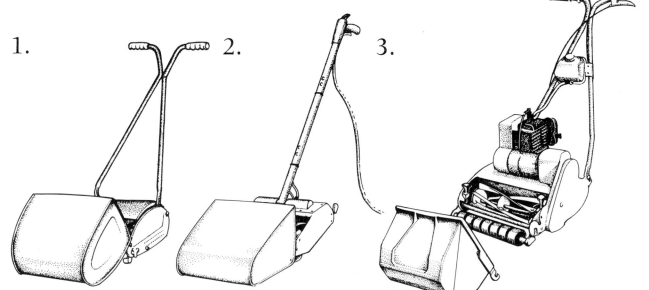

Choosing a mower

The illustrations show the sort of mowers that are most often used for garden lawns. In the table below are some notes on each type to help in the difficult business of selecting the right mower for your garden. Mowers are quite expensive to buy and the most important first step is to choose a machine that will be efficient and reliable for the purposes intended. Too big and expensive a mower may mean cutting the grass more quickly, but it will spend much of its time sitting in the shed. Too small and underpowered a mower can often be thrashed to death in a year or so, trying to do a job it was not meant for. Getting the right balance is important, and the table of mowers' performances will help you to decide. Width of cutting is especially important; 14 inches (350 mm) is a good average for a medium sized lawn.

Type	Area	Frequency. Average cutting height.	Remarks
1. Hand driven cylinder, 10–12 in (250–300 mm) wide	Small lawns, awkward areas.	Weekly in growing season. $\frac{1}{4}$–1 in (6–25 mm)	Convenient, cheap, durable on regularly cut lawns.
2. Electric cylinder. 12–14 in (300–350 mm) wide	Small lawns, awkward areas.	Weekly in growing season. $\frac{1}{4}$–1 in (6–25 mm)	Good on short grass. Cable a constraint. Cheap models lack guts!
3. Petrol cylinder. 12–18 in (300–450 mm)	Medium to large, close mown lawns.	Weekly to fortnightly. $\frac{1}{4}$–1$\frac{1}{4}$ in (6–32 mm)	Robust, efficient and adaptable. The more blades, the better cut. Produces best quality lawns.
4. Petrol rotary. 16–20 in (400–500 mm) wide.	Medium to large lawns and paddock areas.	Weekly to fortnightly – can be left longer. $\frac{3}{4}$–3 in (18–75 mm)	Tough, reliable, versatile. Long and moderately close mown turf. Reasonable quality finish.
5. Petrol rotary hover 16–18 in (400–450 mm) wide	Medium to large lawns and paddocks. Also banks and awkward slopes and beneath hedges, shrubs etc.	Weekly to fortnightly. $\frac{1}{2}$–1$\frac{1}{4}$ in (12–32 mm)	Noisy, effective, but rather shortlived if used heavily. Reasonable finish. Safety important.

4.

5.

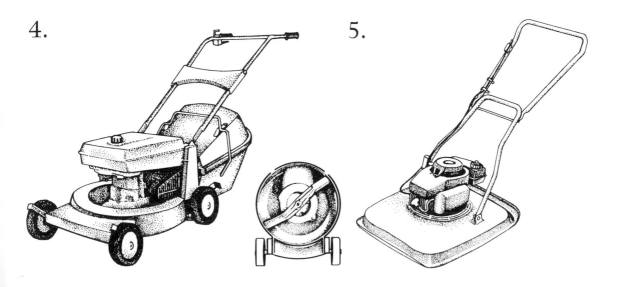

24. Pruning

Pruning is concerned with the control or regulation of the shape and growth of mostly woody plants such as trees, shrubs, hedges and wall plants. The amount of pruning depends very much on the type of woody plants in the garden, the style or character of the design and the actual age and health of the plants.

Obviously for a labour-saving garden the ideal would be no pruning at all, or at least the very minimum to keep everything shapely and healthy, and this within reason is perfectly possible.

Four categories

To understand how we may be able to get away with the minimum of pruning, we must consider four basic categories.

1. Regulation or growth-training of young trees, conifers and shrubs to start them off in the garden with a potentially good shape for their future life. If one starts with well shaped plants from a good nursery then perhaps this stage is really unnecessary.

2. Pruning of deciduous, usually vigorous shrubs to maintain a succession of young healthy growth and flowers or fruit, and to restrict the shape and perhaps promote longevity. In fact, if space is no problem it is possible to be really labour-saving and adopt a let-well-alone policy. After all, in nature shrubs are not usually pruned at all unless it is by browsing animals or wind and exposure. However some, like buddleias, will get far too large, gaunt and leggy if not pruned at some time or another.

So a rational approach is probably advisable if you are growing these types of shrubs.

There are really two categories here:

a. Spring-flowering shrubs that flower on the previous season's wood like forsythias, spiraeas, ribes, lilacs (*Syringa*). When getting large and very twiggy and leggy, prune out old wood and tidy up after flowering – usually in May. Strong cutting-back may also be advisable.

b. Summer-flowering shrubs that flower on new growth made the same season, such as roses, buddleias, fuchsias and caryopteris. When getting too large and leggy, prune hard back in the winter or early spring (see illustration).

There are, however, many more deciduous, slower-growing shrubs like corylopsis, hamamelis, fothergillas, and tree peonies to mention only a few that need no real pruning at all. What could be better, soil permitting, in the labour-saving garden.

3. Evergreen shrubs like camellias, rhododendrons, azaleas, osmanthus, escallonias, ceanothus and many others, need only some light trimming after flowering, and perhaps the removal of dead flower heads or very large or poorly shaped branches.

4. Dwarf, hummock type shrubs or sub-shrubs like brooms, heaths, cistus, lavenders, hebes, salvias and potentillas are best kept in a compact, healthy form by clipping or trimming over after flowering, or in spring; quite an easy job, the sort of thing that the family can do on a nice warm spring day.

When choosing plants for the low-maintenance garden as far as pruning is concerned, concentrate on trees and conifers that normally need little pruning and on those deciduous and evergreen shrubs that also need limited attention in this respect. In actual fact, pruning with a good sharp pair of secateurs is rather an interesting job except, perhaps, in the case of thorny roses or shrubs like berberis and it does not take too long if you adopt a sensible approach and know what you are doing. Clipping everything to symmetrical balls is not the right approach!

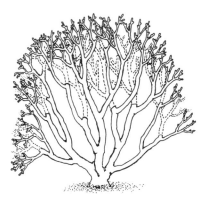

Thin an overgrown shrub to rejuvenate basal growth and form a better shape.

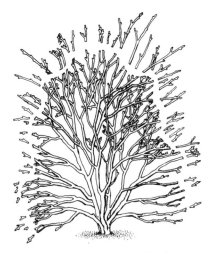

Reduce the size of a large shrub without spoiling its natural effect.

Pruning for health and repair

Another reason for pruning, especially with large mature trees and shrubs, is to remove dead and diseased branches affected by various die-back disorders or perhaps injured by frost or strong winds. In the case of very large trees, you really should consult a reputable specialist or tree surgeon, especially if there is a risk of falling branches damaging people or property next door. The law is fairly clear in this respect and, if you know you have a diseased or potentially dangerous tree which overhangs a neighbour or highway or footpath and if you have clearly not taken steps to avoid this beforehand you will be liable for damage and injury claims. On the other hand, if you were innocent of such advance knowledge and thought the tree to be safe you might not be liable.

Pruning cuts

The textbooks, television and media authorities and other experts advocate very careful pruning cuts to a specific bud with the right angle of cut to deflect rain-water etc. In practice, except in the case of exhibition roses and fruit trees which you are training for special purposes, cutting back with shears or secateurs to an unspecific distance from the main stem without reference to their buds or the angle of the cut seems to work very satisfactorily and for the labour-saving gardener can make the job so much faster. Try it for yourself and see the results.

Pruning tools

Choosing the right tools and keeping them sharp and well maintained is another way of making jobs less arduous and quicker.

Secateurs are an essential tool. Good strong pairs can cut twigs up to ½ in (12 cm) thick without difficulty.

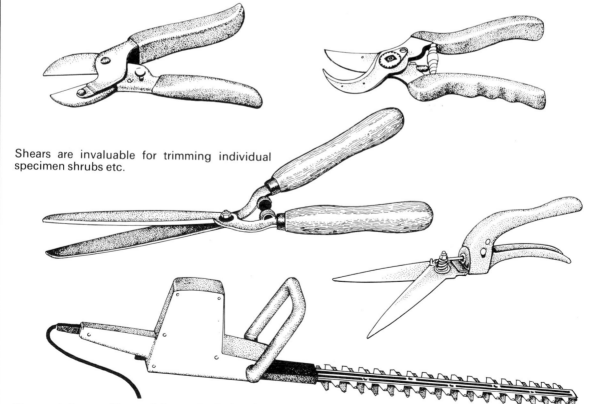

Shears are invaluable for trimming individual specimen shrubs etc.

Powered shears will speed the work of trimming hedges, but it can be a heavy job, particularly with petrol engine models.

25. Pests and Diseases

Pests in particular cover a potentially large group of creatures great and small that can inflict damage or destroy horticultural crops and garden plants. The range includes bulky animals like deer (they can jump 7 ft [2.1 m] fences and love roses), smaller but equally voracious rabbits, and at the other extreme, microscopic mass feeders like aphids and red spiders; all are part of our ecology, living in the countryside, parks and gardens. Then there are diseases and disorders due to fungal rots, mildews and the more complex bacterial and virus problems which cause death, decay or distortion.

In fact very few of this catalogue of pests and plagues need cause serious worry in the average garden where if these problems happen, it will seldom be on an epidemic scale. It is true that in large enterprises, continuous pest and disease control is necessary with large-scale crops of fruit, cereals and vegetables: in these circumstances pests and diseases will increase greatly to match the scale of crops grown. But in gardens there is usually a wide variety of different plants and also most pests have a corresponding number of predators; so a balance is possible. Many small birds eat large numbers of aphids, caterpillars and grubs, so do wasps and hover flies; hedgehogs and slow worms eat slugs and snails and other such pests. It is occasionally that a build-up of pests does happen due to weather or other factors; but even then, invariably, the predators or changes of weather intervene to put a stop to these. So for the labour-saving gardener, the advice here is to encourage the balance in the garden, and to spray or to use chemicals as little as possible.

Nevertheless there will be occasions when even the most relaxed of garden owners in this respect may have to face some unwelcome trouble and therefore a brief résumé is given of those that are most likely to occur in our gardens with some suggestions for remedies.

Pests

Bird damage Birds, especially bullfinches, can strip flowering trees and bushes of buds, especially the plum or cherry group in the early spring, and reference has already been made to the wholesale devouring of fruit crops in the summer. The recently introduced 'humming wires' seem to be having some effect. A cat or two can also be quite discouraging.

Moles have bursts of activity on lawns and in borders, especially on heavy clay soils where they have to keep up a desperate search for worms, their main diet. There are now various cartridge-type repellants available and you can also try setting spiny branches of thorn or gorse in the main runs. Rather unkind this! Others advocate the planting of the caper spurge, *Euphorbia lathyrus*, to discourage moles, though doubt has been cast on its effect.

Slugs and snails can devastate the soft, more tender plants especially in wet spells or in damp locations in mild areas. Pellets are easily scattered among the plants to be protected and a repeat dose should be given after prolonged rainfall.

Aphids, red spiders and caterpillars all appear or disappear from time to time and only when there is a severe occasional infestation of say, aphids on honeysuckles or roses or of blackfly on dahlias do we need to use sprays. The brigade of leaf-suckers and chewers have quite an array of natural predators to deal with and spraying can often upset the balance which can then cause damage to predators. The sort of insecticides to use are the systemic type which are taken up by the plant so that any sucking insect is killed or discouraged when it starts sucking the sap.

A systemic compound is absorbed by a plant and carried in the sap up the stem to all other parts, making the plant itself toxic to pests or pathogens. Its advantage over contact sprays is that you don't have to search for infestations on the plant in order to spray them directly.

Diseases

Honey fungus (*Armellaria mellea*)   This must now be one of the most common and the most destructive fungus diseases in gardens and parks today killing, often quite suddenly, large trees, shrubs and hedges. The illustration shows how it occurs and how it goes about its work and sadly there is no real certain control. Removal of old stumps and infected plants will help. Leave the ground fallow for a time and plant resistant ornamental herbaceous plants. Other species which seem to have some resistance include beech, box, many clematis, elaeagnus, hawthorn, holly, ivy, larch, laurel, mahonia, sumac and yew.

Black spot of roses   This is a very common leaf disease of many garden roses causing defoliation in severe cases. Plant resistant varieties. Suitable floribunda roses are 'Queen Elizabeth', 'Southampton', 'All Gold' and 'Arthur Bell'. Resistant hybrid tea roses include 'Pink Favourite', Silver Jubilee', 'Rose Gaujard', 'Alexander' and 'Peace'. Also, mulch rose beds with a thick layer of fresh lawn clippings or shredded bark to reduce spore movement. Spraying is of course another treatment but it has to be regularly applied, using a suitable fungicide containing benomyl or thiophanate-methyl.

Mildews and moulds on leaves and stems of some garden plants come and go and are related very much to the type of season or conditions. In warm dry weather one tends to get the powdery mildews; in damp warm spells we tend to get more of the downy types. If continuously a problem, perhaps one should scrap the affected plants and grow something more resistant. Spraying with benomyl or thiophanate-methyl is of course another remedy.

Tree diseases causing internal rotting and decay are usually associated with ageing trees, and with damage or water lodging in forked branches. Tree surgeons should be consulted, especially if large trees are seen to have bracket fungi or show discoloured weeping from major branches or parts of the trunk – a sure sign of trouble within.

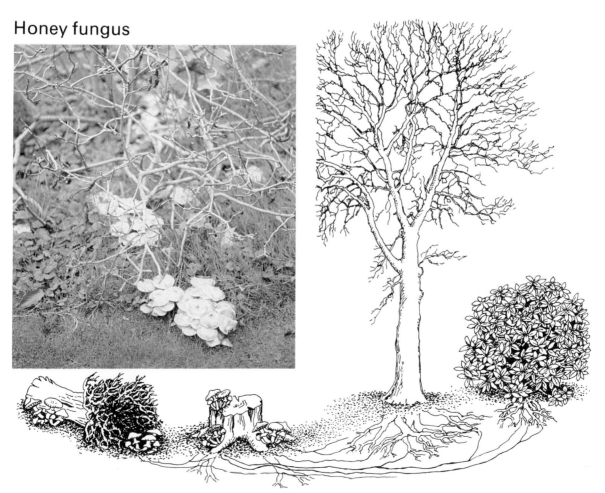

Honey fungus

Honey fungus establishes itself on dead and decaying trees and can be recognised by its buff toadstools. From here it spreads to healthy trees and shrubs by long black 'bootlaces' in the soil.

26. Watering

A sensible approach for all of us these days, whether gardeners or not, is to take account of the need to conserve our water resources, even though we do live on a relatively damp island. In gardens the aim should be wherever possible to conserve water in the soil by mulching and to reduce the number of thirsty exotic plants like some annuals. Hosepipe bans are likely to become more commonplace in the future until a major review of the nation's water resources is contemplated and catered for, and in any case, reducing watering in a garden to the minimum is quite consistent with the labour-saving themes of this book.

Water conservation

We have already seen that the soil-water available to plants in dry spells is mostly held in the organic or humus content and every effort should be made to increase this especially in light sandy soils.

Three ways of conserving water are:

1. Add organic matter into the upper soil layers using rotted manure, mushroom compost, sewage sludge, poultry or horse litter, sawdust, compost, or rotted straw etc. Add additional nitrogenous fertilizers

to encourage the bacterial breakdown of these materials. These are often best applied in late winter or early spring.

2. Apply the organic mulches already described to the surface 3–4 in (7.5–10 cm) thick, adding the nitrogenous fertilizers as above.

3. Gravel or chippings up to 2 in (5 cm) thick are also a means of conserving moisture and they create a clean weed-free surface for certain plants.

1.

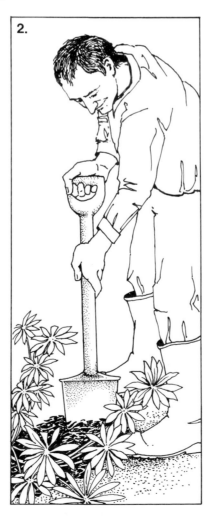

2.

3.

Watering

This is important and at times essential even in the low-maintenance garden, usually in the following situations:

Newly planted trees and shrubs Add peat or compost in the planting pit and soak the root ball at planting and follow with a mulch. In dry spells give each tree at least 2 gallons (9 litres) at each watering. This is normally only necessary in the first year of establishment.

Newly planted perennials, ground-cover etc. These are often best planted in spring, but then liable to suffer in a seasonal drought. Use mulch as before, but water them thoroughly after planting and in dry spells until they are established. After that no more water should be necessary.

Plants in tubs, pots or containers See pages 44–45, and below.

Lawns Even the best turf will go brown in a dry spell. But grasses are amazingly resilient plants and recover very rapidly once the rains come. Therefore, unless the lawn is to be used for a special purpose, I would advocate not watering it at all, certainly as far as this book is concerned.

Rain shadows In small gardens enclosed by high walls or where overhanging gables or eaves of roofs are a feature, locally very dry areas may occur, even during quite wet, or unsettled weather. These permanently dry rain-shadow places may well benefit by the installation of a trickle or lay-flat perforated tubing system fed from a mains supply and turned on from time to time to keep the soil moist.

When applying water, direct the hose or watering-can to the plants that need it. This is preferable to overhead sprinkling. The trickle or drip systems using perforated plastic tubing are also ideal for shrub borders and do save considerable amounts of water as well as placing the water exactly where the plants want it.

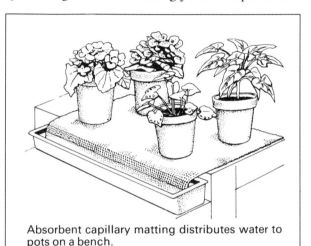

Absorbent capillary matting distributes water to pots on a bench.

Nylon cords will absorb water and deliver it direct into the soil of pots.

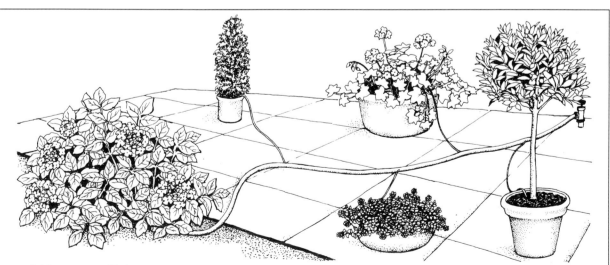

A trickle system of irrigation. Water flows along the hose from the tap and is carried to plants that need regular watering through narrow side tubes.

27. Garden Waste

For the small, labour-saving garden generating very limited quantities of vegetable waste, the simplest means of disposal is to despatch it with all the other waste into the dustbin and thence the refuse cart. There are, however, very many gardens of modest size where quite a quantity of what the ecologists call 'bio-mass', or vegetable bulk, is produced by normal annual growth and some of this is going to be surplus to requirement in the form of weeds, prunings, leaves and lawn clippings. Its disposal can sometimes be both time-consuming and space-demanding.

A year of waste

The following table summarises the average range of garden waste we can expect throughout the year with suggestions for its disposal in the quickest possible manner.

Waste type	Season	Disposal or use
Lawn mowings	Collect during early flush period and at end of season, April and September.	Spread lightly direct on rose or shrub beds as green mulch or add to leaf compost-bins.
Leaves	Mainly October and November.	Collect and pack into net-and-post leaf-bins, or turn into compost.
Prunings, hedge trimmings	Continual production but main peaks in winter, early spring.	Burn (if allowed) – bonfires are always immensely satisfying and can certainly consume large amounts of bulky material. The ashes are useful afterwards for adding to plant beds. Small shredding machines are also available, but they are rather slow to use.
Green weeds	April to November or throughout the year in mild districts or in very weedy gardens.	Catching weeds early with a hoe or herbicides will mean little green material for collection, but where weeds have been allowed to grow and are forming bulky green matter they can be collected and put into mounds and treated with a suitable herbicide. Remove from the garden in the refuse bin.
Household waste	Intermittent throughout the year.	Refuse bin or compost, but beware of rats. Can also be placed in layers in the leaf bin (see illustration).

Leaf bins

A surprising quantity of dried or preferably damp leaves from such trees as beech, hornbeam, oak, sycamore and others can be compressed into fairly compact bins as the illustration shows. Leaves stacked in this way rot down quite speedily without accelerators and can be used one or two years after stacking. Lawn clippings, household waste and ashes can be added to these leaf stacks. Leaves will compress far more readily and rot down faster if they are damp when collected.

Leaf sweeping is often far quicker if done with a large cloth or dust sheet and a splendid gadget called a grabber rake, rather than by using a wheelbarrow. It is often better to wait until most of the leaves have fallen and formed natural drifts in the garden, but do be wary of leaving them lying on lawns too long as they can damage turf.

Two machines for dealing with fallen leaves are illustrated on page 59.

Compost

Much has been written on the correct techniques of making good weed-free garden compost and although it is very commendable to do the job properly, it takes much time, effort and preparation and is not for the labour-saving gardener. Poorly made compost is one sure way of spreading weeds all over the garden! Go for the simple stack of organic waste, layered as far as possible, but do not add weeds when in a seeding state or as living perennials with viable creeping root systems. These sorts of weeds are best stacked separately and drenched with glyphosate or paraquat.

The conifers and low-growing plants of this beautifully planted garden produce comparatively little waste.

28. Tools and Machines

Gardening tools are as ancient as the crafts of gardening itself, instruments fashioned and developed over long periods of time to enable work to be done with less toil, and with more skill and perfection. In more recent times, the advent of powered tools has taken the physical effort out of many jobs to an even greater degree, as well as saving precious time. Today we have at our disposal an impressive array of tools to help in almost every aspect of garden work. A selection is shown here.

In choosing tools think carefully before you buy. Go for those with proven performance, lasting qualities, and capable of the job intended and suited to whoever is going to use them most. Avoid flimsy, novelty gadgets and cheap offers. They are seldom worth it.

Powered tools and machinery are quite expensive, so again choose carefully and always match the machine to the job it is going to do. It should be strong and durable enough to stand up to the hours of work you want it to do, without tiresome and often costly breakdowns. Again, cheap, underpowered, gadgets soon wear out.

Tools for soil cultivation

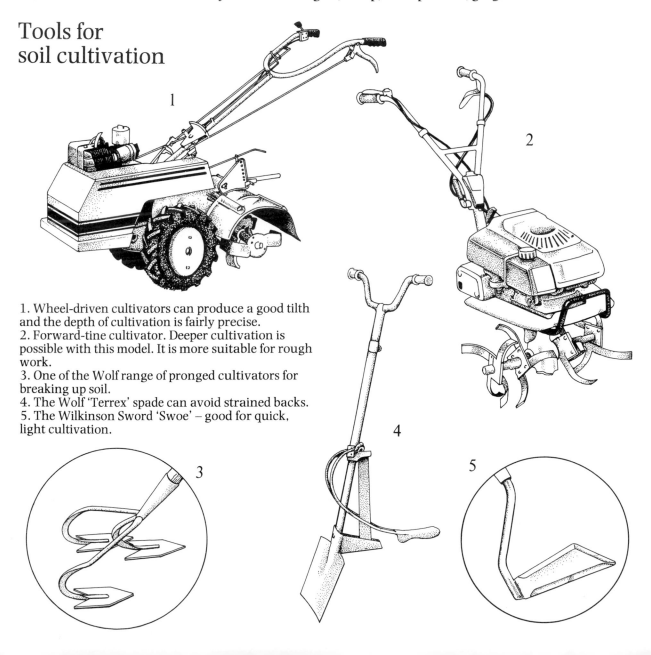

1. Wheel-driven cultivators can produce a good tilth and the depth of cultivation is fairly precise.
2. Forward-tine cultivator. Deeper cultivation is possible with this model. It is more suitable for rough work.
3. One of the Wolf range of pronged cultivators for breaking up soil.
4. The Wolf 'Terrex' spade can avoid strained backs.
5. The Wilkinson Sword 'Swoe' – good for quick, light cultivation.

Tools for lawns

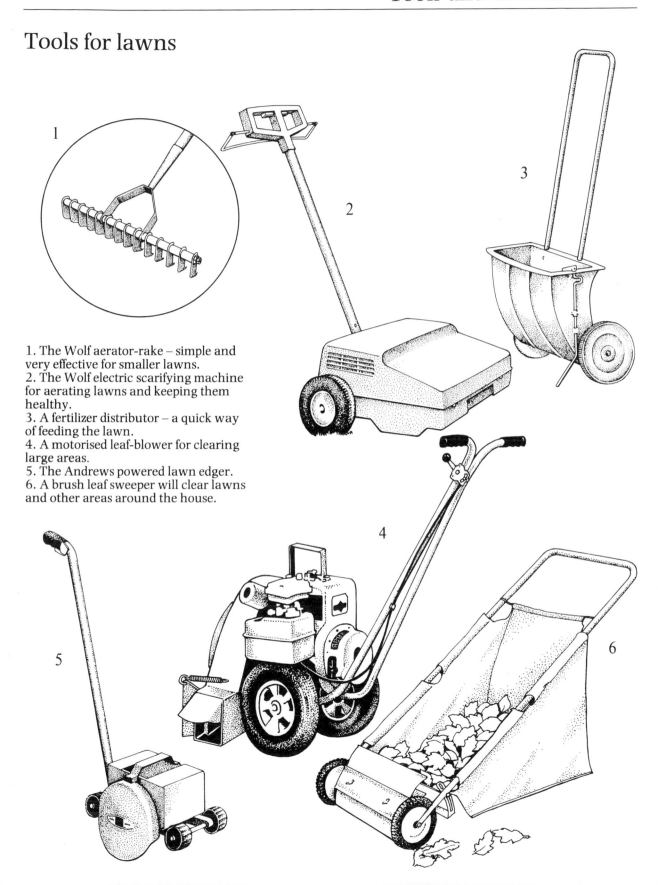

1. The Wolf aerator-rake – simple and very effective for smaller lawns.
2. The Wolf electric scarifying machine for aerating lawns and keeping them healthy.
3. A fertilizer distributor – a quick way of feeding the lawn.
4. A motorised leaf-blower for clearing large areas.
5. The Andrews powered lawn edger.
6. A brush leaf sweeper will clear lawns and other areas around the house.

29. Wild Gardens

Wild gardens are back in fashion again a hundred years after they were first suggested by that great writer and horticulturalist William Robinson. He preached the gospel of the simple beauty of flowers growing naturally, at a period when the Victorian craze for elaborate bedding schemes was at its height.

Today the main reason is probably concerned with the need to preserve nature and wild-life sanctuaries in our gardens and parks, as the countryside becomes more intensively farmed and natural habitats are destroyed; and another reason is perhaps that less maintenance is normally needed for simpler styles of gardening. They can to a certain extent be labour-saving. There are two different types.

1. An informal or wild type garden that may still be used to grow cultivated plants but in a more natural manner.

2. Wild-flower type gardens growing mostly or entirely native plants.

Informal wild gardens

The wild garden in style and character needs to be large enough and in an appropriate setting to look 'wild' and have the right atmosphere; a background of unpruned trees or shrubs is suitable, and even better, a woodland or copse-like setting. If none of these exists they can be created by the right sort of planting, but time and patience will be needed while the trees or shrubs grow. The garden itself can differ in character and can be made up of groups of shrubs or trees in grass allowed to grow longer to meadow length, with access made by closely mown paths running through it; or it can be made up of ground-cover plants, again crossed by natural paths of grass or shredded bark (or neutral coloured gravel in a dry garden). For real labour saving the secret is to associate plants together of a similar character. Apart from weeding in the early years and some annual clipping and possibly grass mowing, there should be

A damp glade in a small woodland garden. Candelabra primulas love these places.

much less maintenance needed. Remember, however, that the effect will be quiet in mood and appearance – softer colours, different textures and shapes, but no real masses of brilliant colours apart from naturalized bulbs in the grass, ground-cover in the spring and perhaps autumn colours from the shrubs. Here are four different examples of wild type gardens to suit the soil, the aspect and the tastes of different labour-saving gardeners:

The Heath Garden   For sandy, acidic soils and an open site. Massed associations of heathers, dwarf rhododendrons and azaleas, ornamental grasses and other heath-type plants and conifers can be arranged naturally in irregularly shaped borders with paths of shredded bark or sawdust. No grass mowing is needed here, but a residual herbicide is used on the paths and the borders are weeded until the plants mass together. Annual clipping is really the only main job. A few well placed birches, maples or other specimen trees will add to the natural effect.

The Chalk Garden   On very dry, chalky or limestone soils and in an open site, associate herbs and shrubs that like these soils such as shrub roses, cistus, daphnes, thymes, sages, rosemary, various vetches, pinks, grey-leafed artemisias and many others. This makes a sort of modified herb garden. Gravel paths or perhaps stepping-stones amongst aromatic ground-cover are recommended, but watch the weeding if this is the case. Similar maintenance is necessary as in the heath garden. A small area of the chalk garden could be set aside for a meadow garden which is described below.

Woodland or Shady Garden   This is associated with groups or copses of suitable trees trimmed up to give a canopy or glade effect and underplanted with ferns, hostas and foxgloves as well as shade-loving shrubs like rhododendrons (if the soil is acidic), flowering dogwoods, Japanese maples and hydrangeas. Bulbs can also be naturalized in ground-cover. If grass is wanted, use a shade mixture and naturalize with species-type crocus, narcissi, hardy cyclamen and autumn crocus. Paths are best made of mown grass or the natural soil, but if likely to be wet, use gravel.

Meadow gardens   In a grassed area, grow a selection of the more vigorous perennial flowers such as daisies

A heath-type wild garden of grasses, low shrubs and perennials.

A meadow garden showing the richness of native flowers in early June.

like rudbeckias, doronicums and chrysanthemums and all kinds of legumes, clovers, vetches, and hardy geraniums. The grass and herbs will be left to grow naturally as a hay meadow and cut in late July and again in September. Bulbs can be naturalized and paths, mown frequently to form winding, tempting trails, will give easier access. Remember that when the long grass is cut in July all the mowings should be removed to keep the character of the hay meadow. To add height and interest, groups or isolated shrubs can be suitably sited to give autumn or spring effects.

A garden of native plants

One has to realise that our wild flowers of the countryside and most of our shrubs are spring- and early summer-flowering, so any garden using these will tend to look its best and most interesting at that time of the year. As the summer goes on and the long grass and vegetation die away, the colours become more of an acquired taste and the adjective 'untidy' is often used by the uninitiated on seeing such a garden for the first time in its off-season state.

Meadow gardens are fascinating to develop from a piece of lawn or by seeding one of the many seed mixtures now available. One secret here is to eliminate the coarser weeds before starting (spot-treat them with a suitable herbicide) and also try to keep the soil fertility as low as possible. On most fertile soils meadow gardens are dominated by the coarser grasses and vigorous weeds. Mowing must be left until late July, when you can use a scythe and should

A dry or gravel garden   Convert a naturally well drained area to such a garden by either covering a weed-free soil with 2–3 in (5–7.5 cm) of gravel or chippings; or by replacing a former lawn, saving all the mowing it involves. Spray it with glyphosate once or twice and then cover it with the gravel. All sorts of plants that like dry stony sites can be planted like Burnet roses, brooms, dwarf willows, spiny-leafed sea hollies and many aromatic plants as well as herbs. Spot treat the gravel with a contact or residual herbicide as necessary.

take away all mowings. Good exercise this and generally labour-saving, once one has achieved the right balance of grasses, herbs and bulbs.

Shaded, woodland-type gardens as already mentioned can also be devoted to native plants and shrubs. Shrubs are important as refuges and food plants for birds, while the herb and grass species are often host plants for many butterflies, moths and insects. In the right wild place, leave patches of nettles, buttercups, willow herbs and even docks and thistles for the same reason. All are splendidly labour-saving in the right place. Cut them down in the spring. Damp or wet places and natural ponds can also be a rich habitat for many attractive waterside or moisture-loving native plants and also for such inhabitants of the ponds as frogs and newts. We do in fact need more ponds now for such creatures as these.

30. Organising the Year

This schedule of the main and unavoidable tasks that have to be completed during the gardening year shows that some of these can be spread more easily in order to ease the load; it also shows the priority needs and the less urgent operations that can be arranged so as to make life less frenzied for the labour-saving gardener. The year has been divided into four quarters.

January to March

Pruning and hedge trimming   This is the best time to do most of the work, especially in dry spells that are likely in early spring. Finish cutting deciduous hedges by the end of March. Leave evergreen or cypress hedges until March or April. Hire or buy mechanical hedge trimmers if you have much hedge cutting to do. Keep pruning/cutting tools in good repair.

Planting   Complete all planting of all open-ground trees, shrubs etc. by end of March. Hedges also. Plants in containers can be left until April for planting out. Don't plant in wet weather or soggy soil conditions.

Weeding   The weather is usually too wet for hoeing; chemicals are the answer here. Use watering-can or pressure bottle-type sprayer or granular type herbicides. Hours of summer weeding can be saved by using chemical herbicides at this time of year. This really can spread the load. Residual chemicals can be used on drives and paths, rose and shrub beds. Contact types can be used in spot treatment on weeds in borders, fruit gardens or fallow ground to catch these late winter-emerging weeds that tend to start growing rapidly in the spring (see also pages 48–49).

Mulches   A good time to spread mulches where appropriate, but preferably apply when the ground is moist. Use fertilizers at the same time.

Spring tidy-up   A good time to trim border plants, shrubby herbs, climbers or others. Remove fallen leaves, branches etc.

Lawns   Turf-laying is possible any time during reasonable weather. Check that the mower is in good shape for the season ahead.

Armchair planning   Not one of the normal pastimes of the labour-saving gardener perhaps, but some advance planning is useful, especially for planting schemes which may mean ordering special trees or plants.

April to June

A very busy time this. Make the most of dry weather spells or the weekend. An important period to work with the weather. Easter holidays are often in the drier April period and if you can set aside one or two good solid gardening days at this critical time or perhaps even taking a half-day off during the week, it can save many hours of work later on – catching up with weeding, late pruning or planting.

Lawn mowing   This becomes a priority throughout this period. Remove clippings from first few cuts only and use as a light mulch on border, rose beds or for composts. A weekly cut is normal in this period and for edges also.

Planting   Perennials, alpines, annuals from containers are best planted in April and May. Seed-sowing outdoors from April onwards. Grass seed can also be sown at this time.

Pruning   Prune spring-flowering shrubs after flowering.

Weed control   When soil begins to dry out and weed seedlings really start to grow, keep the hoe on the move, still a marvellous method of controlling weeds cheaply and economically. An hour's hoeing at the right time can save the long drudgery of hand-weeding later on in the period. Also use chemicals where possible for paths and drives.

Watering   Don't forget newly planted trees, shrubs and the like in very dry spells.

July to September

The holiday season is now upon us, and gardens can stand a few weeks neglect at this time, but not always plants in containers and pots in the glasshouse. If possible arrange friends or neighbours to give the occasional watering and help themselves to vegetables and soft fruit which always seem to be ready when we go on holiday.

Lawn mowing   Reduce cutting frequencies to every other week or much less in dry spells and lift the cutting blade's height; there is no point in scalping lawns in dry weather. Cut long meadow-type grass in late July and remove all mowings.

Weeding   Keep it up, especially before going away.

Pruning/hedges   Some trimming or pruning of spring- or summer-flowering roses, shrubs, climbers etc. at this time. Cut any more vigorous hedges in June or July and yews in August or September.

September to December

The pressure is now easing, the great flush of growth is over and this is a season of dead leaves, dying back of growth and sinking back into armchairs to reflect on the successes and disasters of the last year.

Lawn mowing   Complete mowing usually by late October. Put mower away in a reasonable condition. Seeding lawns in September to early October. Turfing also in this period.

Hedge cutting/pruning   Cut deciduous hedges late in this period or leave until the new year – with the resolutions! Pruning likewise.

Planting   Plant conifers and perennials while weather is still good. Trees etc. later on.

Leaves   Leaves will be everywhere from October onwards. Remove at least from lawns as quickly as possible and use for mulches or compost.

Index

T. W. J. Wright is Senior Lecturer in Landscape and Amenity Horticulture at Wye College, University of London. His writings include articles on garden maintenance and volume IV of *The Gardens of Britain – The Gardens of Kent, Sussex and Surrey*.